GOLD RUSH

Cover photographs by Ian and Sally Wilson
*Front Cover: Ian Wilson riding across the Little
Tahltan River on the Stikine Trail.*
*Back Cover: Approaching the Five Finger Rapids
on the Yukon River in a hand-built scow.*

Our sincere thanks to:

*Altamira Investment Services
Hastings Management
Richard Hughes
Klondike Gold Corp.
Molson Breweries*

*for their generous support
of our Klondike expedition*

GOLD RUSH

**Reliving the Klondike Adventure
in Canada's North**

Text and Photographs by

Ian & Sally Wilson

Illustrations by Sally Tatlow Wilson

Gordon Soules Book Publishers Ltd.
West Vancouver, Canada
Seattle, USA

With special thanks to Maureen Colclough for all her help with this book

First printing August, 1996
Second printing September, 1996

Published in Canada by
Gordon Soules Book Publishers Ltd.
1354-B Marine Drive
West Vancouver, BC
Canada V7T 1B5

Published in the U.S.A. by .
Gordon Soules Book Publishers Ltd.
620 - 1916 Pike Place
Seattle, WA 98101

Canadian Cataloguing in Publishing Data
Wilson, Ian, 1955 –
Gold rush

Includes bibliographical references and index
ISBN 0-919574-59-9

1. Wilson, Ian, 1955–   2. Wilson, Sally, 1955–
3. Frontier and pioneer life—Yukon Territory.
4. Frontier and pioneer life—British Columbia, Northern.
5. Klondike River Valley (Yukon)—Description and travel.
6. British Columbia, Northern—Description and travel.
7. Klondike River Valley (Yukon)—Gold discoveries.
I. Wilson, Sally, 1955– II. Title.
FC4017.3W54 1996   917.19'1043   C96-910298-4
F1095.K5W54 1996

Edited by Anne Norman
Cover design by Harry Bardal
Typeset by CompuType Graphics, Vancouver, BC, Canada
Printed and bound in Canada by Best Book Manufacturers

CONTENTS

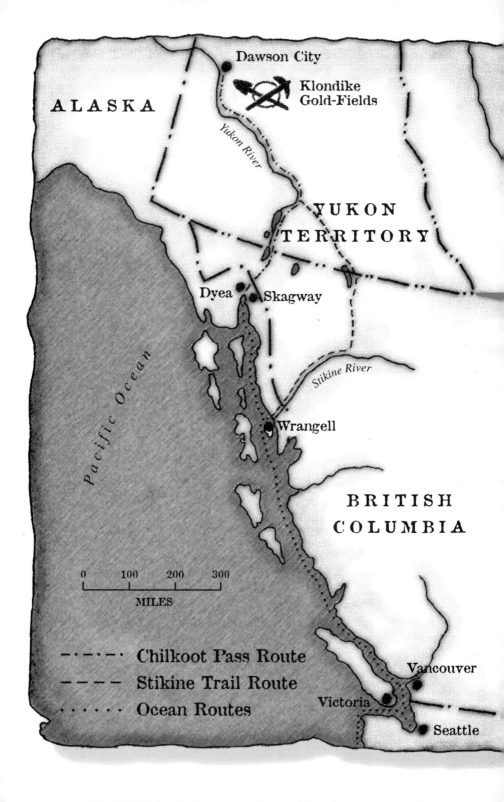

DAWSON CITY

Klondike
Gold-Fields

ALASKA

Yukon River

YUKON
TERRITORY

Dyea

Skagway

Stikine River

Pacific Ocean

Wrangell

BRITISH
COLUMBIA

0   100   200   300
MILES

—·—·—·— Chilkoot Pass Route
— — — Stikine Trail Route
· · · · · Ocean Routes

Vancouver

Victoria

Seattle

DOMINION OF CANADA

Map
OF THE
Chilkoot
— AND —
Stikine
Routes
TO THE
Klondike

1 8 9 7

Sally Wilson
1996

GOLD IN THE KLONDIKE!

— ⋈◊⋈ —

THE RECENT reports from the Yukon of marvellous discoveries of gold of untold richness would seem incredible were it not for the hundreds of sacks of "dust" taken from the placers of the far North, which returned miners are bringing back with them.

A TON AND A HALF OF GOLD!

— ⋈◊⋈ —

Sixty-eight passengers on a North American Transportation & Trading Company's steamship recently reached civilization from the far north. The passengers were mostly miners, direct from the Klondike placer mining districts. The men brought back one and one-half tons of gold in nuggets and dust, worth more than $1,000,000.

This news from the Klondike will no doubt tempt scores of hardy and adventurous spirits to seek a fortune in the frozen North!

JULY 1897

*What a would-be Klondiker
might have read a century ago.*

ONE

The Klondike Spirit

A century has passed since the first cry of "Gold in the Klondike" echoed around the world, drawing people north to the Yukon with the promise of riches and adventure. Even today, the Klondike spirit grips people and does not let go.

Sally and I can attest to the power of the spell. It took us from our chairs in the Vancouver library one January afternoon to the Yukon—to a place where gold, new experiences, and open space seemed limitless.

While looking for a good book for rainy-day reading, I had come across an old Yukon diary. The firsthand account of the gold rush of 1897–1898 and the story of the great stampede north started me dreaming about a trip to the gold-fields.

"That's it," I said to Sally after reading several pages. "How about the Klondike for our next adventure?"

Sally snapped her book closed and looked up with a smile. "Sounds good to me!" she said, as if I'd proposed a picnic at the local park. She leaned across the table and turned the book around to see what I'd been reading.

I'd had a hunch that Sally would be enthusiastic. After all, we had made a career of exploring Canada's wilderness and sharing our experiences through our writing and slide presentations. Actually, "career" is not quite the right word. Sally and I had long ago discovered that we were drawn to wild places, particularly in the north. For the past decade, books and slide shows were our way of supporting our passion for the outdoors.

Our first extended trip had taken us to an isolated valley in northern British Columbia where we built a log cabin and lived for a year. On another journey, we travelled to remote wilderness areas to photograph wildlife through four seasons. And when the need to seek new horizons surfaced again, Sally and I chose the Arctic. We canoed across the Barrens, lived with an Inuit family, then travelled by dog team along the coast of Hudson Bay.

Now it looked as if the Klondike would lure us to the north again. Sally and I tested the idea by poring over books about the gold rush, and we were soon captivated by the old photographs. Some images became so familiar as we encountered them in book after book that the people in them began to seem more like relatives than strangers from long ago.

One person in particular caught our attention each time we saw his photograph. He was a whiskered prospector bound for the Klondike gold-fields, holding a shovel and a pickaxe in his hands. Pots, pans, blankets, and a gold pan dangled from his pack-board. A broad-rimmed miner's hat framed his face, but it was his eyes that we noticed most. They showed such determination. His whole demeanour suggested a sense of purpose that inspired us.

"I've already nicknamed this guy 'Iron Grip,' " Sally said. "It looks as though he won't let go of that shovel until he's dug for gold in the Yukon."

We eagerly read old newspaper clippings, Klondikers' journals, and even their lists of supplies. With each book we read, our plans began to take shape. Pictures showed gold-seekers leading packhorses, trekking up mountain passes, and floating down rivers. There was no way we could go back in time and participate in the human stampede to the gold-fields, but we thirsted for a chance to find out what it had been like.

Among the half-dozen routes taken to the Yukon, we searched for one that would fulfil our quest for adventure and our desire to follow in the footsteps of Klondikers from a century before. The most popular means of getting to the Klondike had been to travel by ship along the west coast to Alaska, then trek over the Chilkoot Pass or White Pass. But as we looked at different routes, the Stikine Trail through northern British Columbia stood out as being unchanged since the gold rush. It was still a faint path through remote wilderness, and we felt it would best duplicate the experiences of the stampeders.

I came across another photograph of people leading packhorses and my thoughts turned to a horseback trip. Even though I had little experience with horses other than watching western movies, I had often thought about travelling by packhorse. Now, I suggested to Sally that this way of travel should be part of our journey. My words must have been pretty convincing. We made the hasty and romantic decision to try to retrace the all-Canadian route along the Stikine Trail with horses.

When Sally resumed reading, I closed my eyes. The *clip-clop* of a library patron's shoes became a string of obliging packhorses that Sally and I were guiding along a mountain trail. I imagined a dusty, open trail, azure skies, and friendly steeds named Rusty and Trusty.

Sally's hand on my arm brought me back to the present.

"The Stikine Trail only goes partway. We'll have to build a boat and float down the Yukon River, just as they did a hundred years ago," she said. I was still thinking about horses, and had trouble visualizing this new part of our journey.

To convince me, Sally read an account of a Klondiker who had joined the flotilla of rough-hewn boats that drifted down the river. The way the writer described it, the journey had been a fabulous enterprise with roller-coaster rapids and the camaraderie of fireside companions.

"Ah, it seems you missed the bit about how many of those

boats sank," I said, looking over her shoulder.

"I did? It must have been an oversight," Sally replied mischievously. Hardly taking a breath, she began reading another story about floating down the Yukon River.

Before long, I became intrigued by the idea of following their oar-strokes towards the gold-fields. Both of us were captivated by photographs showing stampeders sailing along lakes and careening down rapids. Floating downriver to Dawson City in our own hand-built scow, sipping tea under hand-stitched sails, boldly going where no sane landlubber would ever go—now, that was the life!

As Sally and I schemed and dreamed, we began to grasp how far it was to the gold-fields and how long our journey would take. The Stikine Trail would not be free of snow until mid-June and it would take us five or six weeks to follow the route with horses. Then we would need a couple of weeks to build a scow, and another four weeks to float to Dawson.

"It looks like it will be nearly winter by the time we get to Dawson. So, when do we look for gold?" Sally asked. I thought I detected the first symptoms of gold fever: rapid breathing and a faraway look in her eyes.

"I guess we should spend the winter and find our gold the next summer," Sally added with as much confidence as any stampeder. Now I knew she had gold fever! But the stampeders would have had every reason to be confident. Back then, newspapers had promoted the idea that gold was available to anyone with a pick and shovel. According to reports, all a person had to do to strike it rich was get to the gold-fields. The more old newspapers Sally and I read, the more we believed it ourselves.

All our trips seemed to start this way, with modest beginnings that grew to epic proportions along the way. I had a feeling that this trip would be no different. Each time we read an account of a gold-seeker who tackled the passes, the rivers, and the winter trails, some of the Klondike spirit rubbed off on us. With increasing enthusiasm, we added a snowshoe trip and gold mining to our wish-list for a well-rounded Klondike experience.

Our next step was to visit the map store to see if our planned route was feasible. As with our previous journeys, the gathering of maps brought the trip a step closer to reality, at least on paper.

"Come and look at this," Sally called. She had unrolled one of the maps for the horseback portion of our trip. "The old Stikine Trail is still marked on these maps!"

I followed her finger as she traced a dotted line across two rivers and up a steep mountainside. A long section of the trail was missing, obliterated by the hatch marks that indicated swamp and bog.

"That might be a problem," Sally said.

I countered with unfounded optimism. "Nah," I replied. "Even if the trail isn't marked any more, we'll find it. The old maps will show where it used to be." Hasty words!

Just past the halfway point, the trail came to an abrupt end on current maps. From there we planned to take a parallel trail that led to Atlin, a route used during the later days of the gold rush. Even that route had several disconcerting sections where no trail was shown.

"The first blank spot is only the length of my hand," Sally said flippantly, as she looked at the map. My earlier optimism must have been contagious. We both knew the span of a hand represented several days worth of wasteland that we would have to push through to reach Atlin. From there, Sally and I would continue towards Whitehorse. Then we would sell our horses and build a scow to float downriver to Dawson City.

In the comfort of the map office, the plan looked quite straightforward. We left with a bundle of thirty-two maps to cover our nine-hundred-mile trip.

"Now that we know where we're going, we'll need a gold pan and some advice on prospecting," Sally suggested. Armed with a list of supplies that had been recommended by a newspaper in 1897, we made our way to an outfitter's store.

"The bigger the gold pan the more gold you'll find," the whiskered outfitter said with a smile when he learned of our plans. "And I'd use a metal pan. One of those newfangled plastic ones might buckle under the weight of your gold."

Sally missed the conspiring wink directed at me. She selected the largest gold pan on the shelf, one that resembled an oversized frying pan without a handle. Meanwhile, the outfitter handed me a folding shovel and a pickaxe.

"You'll need a gold poke. In fact, make that two," he added, holding up a pair of small leather pouches. As he continued with a long list of gold-mining paraphernalia we felt as bewildered as any would-be Klondikers must have felt years ago.

Through our reading, we learned that most people heading to the Yukon had no idea what to take for a year-long trip in the cold north. They had to rely on advice from the sudden abundance of outfitters and advertisements that had appeared after news of the gold strike. The more gullible gold-seekers bought Klondike folding boats that didn't float and Klondike bicycles that would never negotiate the mud-bottomed trails. Other stampeders bought mechanical gold pans that supposedly took the work out of finding gold.

"I think you should outfit yourselves the way the Klondikers did," the old-timer suggested when he saw me eyeing a traditional pack-board displayed on the wall. For a moment, I thought he was going to pull out a folding boat. When he started telling tales of cooking over open fires and sleeping in canvas tents, we warmed to the idea. Sally and I decided that, like the old days, we would sleep in a canvas tent and wear old-style oilskin jackets and hats. We would even cook our meals in enamel cookware.

"If you really want the flavour of pioneer life, your menu should include beans, bacon, and bannock," he added. Sally liked that idea, but my suggestion that we use our gold pan for a plate, mixing bowl, baking tin, and wash basin didn't catch on as easily.

Sure enough, when we reread the provision lists from 1897, we found that most were heavy on the beans and bannock.

"According to this, one person's supply of beans for a year weighs almost as much as I do. I'm not that keen on beans,"

A MINER'S OUTFIT

PROVISIONS BEING CALCULATED UPON THE QUANTITY
SUFFICIENT TO MAINTAIN ONE MAN FOR ONE YEAR

8 Sacks Flour
150 lbs. Bacon
150 lbs. Split Peas
150 lbs. Beans
25 lbs. Evaporated Apples
25 lbs. Evaporated Peaches
25 lbs. Apricots
25 lbs. Butter
100 lbs. Granulated Sugar
1 1/2 doz. Condensed Milk
15 lbs. Coffee
10 lbs. Tea
1 lb. Pepper
10 lbs. Salt
8 lbs. Baking Powder
40 lbs. Rolled Oats
2 doz. Yeast Cakes
1/2 doz. 4 oz. Beef Extract
5 bars Castile Soap
6 bars Tar Soap
1 tin Matches
1 gal. Vinegar
1 box Candles
25 lbs. Evaporated Potatoes
25 lbs. Rice
25 Canvas Sacks
1 Wash Basin
1 Medicine Chest
1 Rubber Sheet
1 set Pack Straps
1 Pick and extra Handle
1 Shovel
1 Gold Pan
1 Axe and extra Handle
1 Whip Saw

1 Hand Saw
1 Jack Plane
1 Brace
4 Bits, assorted, 3/16 to 1 in.
1 8-in. Mill File
1 Broad Hatchet
1 2-qt. Galv'd Coffee Pot
1 Fry Pan
1 Package Rivets
1 Draw Knife
3 Cov'd Pails
1 Pie Plate
1 Knife and Fork
1 Granite Cup
1 each Tea and Table Spoon
1 14-in. Granite Spoon
1 Tape Measure
1 1/2-in. Chisel
10 lbs. Oakum
10 lbs. Pitch
5 lbs. 20d. Nails
5 lbs. 10d. Nails
200 feet 5/8in. Rope
1 Single Block
1 Solder Outfit
1 Pair Rowlocks
1 14-qt. Galvanized Pail
1 Granite Saucepan
3 lbs. Candle Wick
1 Compass
1 Candle Stick
6 Towels
1 Axe Stone
1 Emery Stone

☞ HO FOR THE KLONDIKE! ☜

1897

*A list a would-be Klondiker
might have used a century ago.*

I protested. There was an equal weight of bacon, and even more flour. The lists weren't very imaginative.

"Here's a list we can live with," Sally replied, running her finger down a page in a gold-rush guidebook. It had considerably more variety, including peas, condensed milk, tinned ham, dried fruits, and vegetables.

Dried food was a big seller then, from dehydrated onions, to coffee lozenges and beef cubes. A walnut-sized cube of concentrate was advertised to "provide enough soup for ten hungry men." We scanned the lists, trying to imagine what it had been like to shop for a year's supply of such provisions. We also wondered where we could buy the magic soup cubes these days.

"I found a better list—this is the one for us!" Sally said a while later, waving a page at me. "It includes eight pounds of chocolate."

We continued planning and packing, and by early March our pile of goods was so large that we had to rent a storage locker. It wasn't long before the locker was bursting at the seams with food and equipment for our trip.

"We're definitely approaching the ton of goods that the stampeders were required to have," I said as I stacked another box on the pile. The locker was cluttered with ropes, a canvas tent, packsaddles, and boxes. There were piles of winter clothing and summer clothing, as well as boxes and boxes of dried food.

The next day we went shopping for our riding outfits and visited almost every used tack shop in the Vancouver area. As I turned into the driveway of Budget Tack, Sally heaved a heavy sigh. She hates shopping.

"Come on," I encouraged. "I saw a pair of cheap chaps here yesterday and thought they might fit you."

I found a pair of used riding chaps for myself as well and emerged from behind a rack to model them. "Do these fit?" I asked the salesperson.

"Well," she said slowly, looking me up and down, "have you ridden much before?"

"Not much."

"I thought that might be the case," she continued, still eyeing me critically. "You've got them on backwards."

How embarrassing! Obviously, we were greenhorns. To my untrained eye, the chaps were merely two identical leather leggings attached to straps on a belt.

"We don't know much about saddles either. Could you tell us what a sixteen-inch-quarter-horse-cross-bar is?" That was the type of saddle we had been told to buy.

She was still chuckling when she pulled a binder onto the countertop. "This is where the measurements are taken," she said, opening to a full-page illustration. She pointed to the front of the saddle.

"And you can leave off the 'cross' part. It's just a quarter-horse bar," she added. She didn't have any saddles for us, but we left with our chaps and a woven band of string, called a cinch, for a saddle.

Small details began to bog us down at this stage. What type of rigging was used for packsaddles? What kind of caulking was suitable for our scow? Would a toboggan or a Yukon sled be better for the winter trip? Each question elicited a different answer from the people we asked and the books we read.

Our best source of information was a tattered old guidebook titled *Gold Fields of the Klondike* by Ernest Ingersoll. In addition to lists of gear required for a Klondike expedition, he'd advised: "Ample provision must be made for the boat and sled construction, which is a feature of every journey overland. To this end these items will be absolutely necessary: one jack-plane, one whipsaw, one axe and one measuring rule . . ." The list also recommended a selection of nails and screws, a roll of oakum, and a can of pitch. With the guidebook in hand, we set off to visit ship chandlers and old-style hardware stores to buy more supplies.

By the time we added the boat-building supplies to the piles of food and gear in the locker, we were well on our way to being outfitted for the Klondike. Now all we had to do was learn how to ride, pack, and shoe horses, and figure out how to build a scow.

TWO

Learning the Ropes

Spurred by the gold rush, boat-building demonstrations and gold-panning lessons were available in almost every city up and down the west coast in 1897. There were even horse-packing clinics where gold-seekers could learn the diamond hitch, said to be the only way to hold a load on a horse's back.

These days, Sally and I couldn't find even one school in downtown Vancouver offering the basics for would-be Klondikers. However, we did find a horse-packing clinic offered by Jim McCrae in Aldergrove, only an hour's drive from the city. When Jim invited us out to his farm, Sally and I quickly decided to leave boat building, shoeing, and riding lessons until later.

We arrived at Jim's armed with a long list of questions. Actually, we were overwhelmed by the things we didn't know and we were beginning to have some doubts about the trip. Several horse people had offered endless reasons why we shouldn't go: the route was too long and difficult, the horses would starve unless we brought a staggering supply of oats, and we would need to be accompanied by a farrier. And most disturbing of all to them—we were greenhorns.

On that first meeting Jim spent the whole afternoon answering many of our questions. To our relief, Jim's comments were all positive. If he thought we couldn't do the trip, he kept those thoughts under his broad-rimmed hat.

"Forget cowboy boots," was his first suggestion after reviewing our list. "Hiking boots are essential for walking— and you'll be doing a lot of that. Just make sure they have a good heel so they won't slide right through the stirrups."

Jim helped us decide on other types of clothing and gear for the horseback trip. He also offered to teach us how to tie the double-diamond hitch.

"The double diamond is a favourite with shorter people because they don't have to reach the top of a load to tie the knots," he explained.

"Why don't we start on this horse?" Jim suggested. I looked around, but saw only a large fuel barrel perched on four metal legs.

"This appaloosa is the calmest cayuse you'll ever load," Jim said with a chuckle, patting the steel steed, which was painted black with white spots. On this "horse" we learned how to place the padding and packsaddle in the correct position to avoid injuring the horse. Once the saddle was cinched tightly, we added pack-boxes and bulky bags to simulate the load our horses would carry. Then Jim threw a canvas tarp over the works.

In just over a minute, Jim magically transformed a long coil of rope into the double-diamond hitch by performing a series of twists, turns, and loops. I had a feeling it would take Sally and me considerably longer.

"I'll slow down a little so you can pick up the moves," Jim said, untying the rope. After he had tied the hitch three more times, it was our turn. I was glad Sally and I could work together because I wasn't sure if I would be able to remember the complex sequence of knots and contortions.

To start the hitch, Sally secured one end of the rope to a cinch ring and pulled a long loop of rope through the ring. She passed the loop over the top of the barrel to me.

I hooked the loop to my end of the cinch under the barrel,

and Sally pulled the rope tight. It took a few minutes of hemming and hawing before Sally sent the rope over the front of the "horse" to me. With Jim's help, I worked the rope through several twists and turns on my side. When I pulled the rope tight, a diamond-shaped web of rope appeared on the side of the load.

"Here, Sal," I said, passing the rope over the back of the load. When she pulled everything tight, a diamond formed on her side as well.

"Whew, I wonder if we can do that again?" Sally asked, admiring our handiwork. Our first attempt had taken twenty minutes. After several hours of practice and more tangled rope than I care to remember, we cut our time down to a more respectable ten minutes.

Repeating the process on a real horse was much more challenging. This horse moved! It stepped nimbly aside when we attempted to load the boxes. It tried to nip me as I looped the rope over its withers. It stomped on my boot as I leaned close to tie a knot. Luckily, Jim offered to spend more time with us until we could tie the hitch without tying ourselves in knots.

By mid-March Sally and I had mastered the diamond hitch, but we were still missing a most important ingredient—horses. Without them, the first part of our journey to the gold-fields would be impossible. I contacted our friends, Ray and Reg Collingwood in northern British Columbia. They were guides and outfitters and quickly offered to put us in touch with a wrangler named Slim. After telling Slim our plans, I asked if he could find four or five horses for us by the middle of May.

"I think the horses should be experienced, because we're not," I explained, hoping that he could find calm, gentle creatures for us. Sally and I also wanted trail-wise bush horses that were accustomed to being enveloped by clouds of bugs while crossing swamps with no trails to follow. Slim agreed to select horses that greenhorns like us could handle.

"Not too big," I cautioned when Slim suggested strong, large-boned horses. I couldn't see myself or Sally heaving loaded pack-boxes up onto a moose-sized creature.

"Are there any particular problems we should prepare for?" I asked.

"You mean other than your horses running away or a load falling off?" Slim asked. There was a long silence over the phone while I pondered those scenarios.

"Well, somewhere along the way a horse will lose a shoe," Slim said finally. "You can count on it!" He reminded me that horses couldn't go without shoes because rough trails would wear down their hoofs.

Leaving Slim to find horses in Smithers, we continued our preparations in Vancouver. With his advice in mind, we returned to the library to learn about horseshoeing. Sally and I agreed that she would be most likely to succeed with horseshoeing—after all, she still had a hoof pick from her Pony Club days when she was ten years old. I wasn't sure how comfortable I would feel sitting on top of a horse, never mind crouching underneath one. Equipment repair and horse first aid would be my contributions.

"I can hammer nails," Sally said to me as she read through a horseshoeing manual. "It can't be that difficult to nail shoes onto a horse's foot, can it?"

But as Sally read further, the furrows on her brow deepened. Finally, she looked over to me. "Maybe this isn't going to be quite as easy as I'd thought."

"Listen to this," she said, referring to a sheaf of notes and diagrams piled on her lap. "Driving the nails into the horse's hoof is a great concern to beginners. It is the most dangerous part of horseshoeing as far as potential damage to the horse."

"Doesn't that book say anything encouraging?" I asked. "Maybe we should look in a different section of the library—like the 'how-to books for optimists' section."

Sally scanned the pages. "Well, it more or less says that if you follow the directions closely and get plenty of practice, you can't go wrong."

"Sounds good. Now all we have to do is find someone who will let us hammer nails into their horse's feet," I said.

After many enquiries we met a willing instructor, farrier

Don Knapp. When we arrived at his stable, Don greeted us with a warm handshake and a real horse—with real legs and real hoofs.

"After hearing about your other trips, I'm keen to help you with this one. Anyone who can build a cabin should be able to shoe a horse." Sally glanced over at me and flashed a smile of relief. I could tell that she felt encouraged by these words.

"I've been thinking about how to simplify things," Don continued, while scratching his horse's neck. "And I've decided to teach you only what you need to know."

We watched closely as Don demonstrated the art of trimming and filing a front hoof and nailing on a shoe. Then it was Sally's turn. She handed me the halter rope with instructions to hold the horse steady while she worked.

Don made sure that Sally was in the proper stance with knees bent so that her back wasn't overworked as she placed the hoof between her knees.

"Point your toes in more and keep your knees together. They create a platform to support the hoof," he said.

"Will the horse bite me?" I interrupted, backing away as the horse nudged me.

"No," Don answered with a laugh. Meanwhile, Sally was struggling to keep her balance as the horse moved. Don suggested that if I kept the horse's head a little to the other side, it would take some weight off the leg Sally was supporting.

"Sally, hold that file lightly," he instructed, prying loose her fingers to release her grip. "Just drag it across, otherwise you'll take too much off the hoof."

Soon it was time to nail on the shoe—the moment Sally had been dreading.

"Where's the white line I've been reading about?" Sally asked. She was studying the hoof hesitantly.

"That's it there," Don said as Sally rubbed a finger along the faint line.

"Remember to set the bevel so the nail gets driven out the hoof wall. Then you can bend it back over," he cautioned. Sally checked the square-sided nail for the third time.

Tap . . . tap . . . tap. It was a feeble effort, not what I expected of Sally. Her knees were shaking under the weight of the horse. She let go of the nail and it fell to the ground.

"Why don't you take a break," Don suggested. Both Sally and the horse stretched their backs and legs, shifting from foot to foot. After a few minutes Sally started again. This time Sally swung the hammer with more confidence.

"It looks good," Don encouraged. "If you hit it hard now, the bevel will drive the nail out." It did.

"Bend the nail over as soon as it's through," Don added urgently. "If he pulls his foot away that nail could rip your leg open."

I stroked the horse's neck to keep him calm as Don had suggested. By the third nail, I noticed that the horse was no longer trembling and guessed that Sally wasn't either. Things were coming along nicely. That was, until Sally started the fourth nail.

"This angle doesn't look right," Sally said anxiously, leaning to one side for Don to see.

"Just hit it hard and it'll come out."

After one firm rap, the nail head was set in the shoe but the point didn't come through the hoof wall. It was somewhere inside the soft inner hoof, in a network of a million tiny blood vessels.

Sally went pale. "Pull the nail out, Don!" she pleaded. As Sally tensed, the horse began trembling again. Luckily, Don remained calm and showed Sally how to use the clippers to pull the nail. Then he handed her another nail.

Eventually, Sally learned to trust her hunches, pulling out the nails or driving them in with confidence. Once the first shoe was on, Sally gave her work a critical scrutiny. The nails weren't in a tidy row like Don's, yet they had all emerged in an acceptable pattern. That shoe would not work its way loose.

It took Sally two more hours to file down and shoe the other two hoofs.

As we left the stable, I turned to Sally. "I think we handled that pretty well, especially the horse-holding part," I said, quite proud of myself.

Loading a horse

Horseshoeing practice

Sally gave me a sideways glance. "Well, that's good to hear. I need just a bit more practice shoeing before our trip, though."

I held up one foot. "You can practise on mine," I offered.

"No thanks. A horse would be calmer," she said, waving an intimidating pair of arm-long hoof clippers towards me.

With a good start on horseshoeing, Sally and I discussed what our next step should be.

"Let's take gold-panning lessons now," Sally suggested, rubbing her hands together with exaggerated eagerness.

"Take a pill for that gold fever," I returned, placing a hand on her forehead to check her temperature. "We have to get to the Klondike first. And speaking of getting there, I think I should learn how to ride a horse."

My only horseback experience was a one-hour dude ride as a child. If I remember correctly, I was lifted into the saddle and the horse was pointed down a loop trail, following several other horses. All I had to do was hang on to the horn with two hands; the horse was on auto pilot. Somehow, I don't think that hour counted much towards being a rider. Sally reminded me that her riding had earned a Pony Club blue ribbon when she was ten, but she would join me in riding lessons anyway to brush up on her skills.

I spent hours working my way through the telephone book, calling riding stables in the Greater Vancouver area. Because we were novices, I was told there was not enough time before our departure to learn the skills required for our long horseback expedition.

"I doubt the stampeders had to deal with this kind of response," I quipped to Sally.

"You've got a point there," she said. "From what I've read, everyone would have been encouraging us with a hearty 'Ho for the Klondike!'"

Our luck changed when I reached the *M*'s. At Mustang Riding Stables, Italo answered the phone. As I described our plans, he became excited by the challenge of helping us prepare for the trip. Although it was already early April, Italo felt confident he could teach us the basics of horseback riding before we headed north.

We arrived at the stable suited-up in our chaps, new hats, and leather riding gloves, ready for our first outing. Italo had other plans.

"Before you jump into the saddle, you have to learn about horses," he said. He began by showing us how to lead a horse safely and where to stand when working on or near a horse.

"You have to establish your dominance," he explained. "Horses will try to get away with anything. And when an animal the size of a horse misbehaves, it can compromise your safety."

Like Don Knapp, Italo had worked out a plan to teach us the most important skills. Over the next few visits, we learned to saddle, groom, and care for the horses. As I learned how to ride and handle horses, I overcame my apprehension of working with these large animals. I learned how to bandage legs, treat injuries, and give oral medications and intramuscular injections. With Italo's help, we assembled a horse first-aid kit that was suitable for our extended trip.

Sally and I had just returned from our last riding lesson when Slim phoned from northern British Columbia to say that we now owned three horses. On our behalf, Slim had purchased two geldings, aged eight and eighteen. The other horse was a five-year-old mare.

Three horses were a good start, but we still had to find another horse or two. We needed one each to ride and one each to pack our loads. Ideally, we'd take an extra horse as well, but Slim reported he was having trouble finding any others at a reasonable price.

I was surprised to learn that horses were nearly as difficult to come by now as they had been for stampeders a hundred years ago. Back then, horses sold for six or seven times what they had been worth before the gold rush. Any sway-backed, bow-legged steed had been deemed fit for the trail. I realized that even our standards were dropping somewhat when I saw Sally eyeing a large dog in the neighbourhood, as if sizing it up for a pack.

For the time being, Sally and I had done all we could to prepare for the horseback part of our trip. We would be travelling only partway by horse, and now we turned our attention to the second half of our journey. Like the stampeders, we would float down the Yukon River to get to the gold-fields. After studying Klondikers' diaries, we decided that a sturdy, box-shaped scow would be the craft for us. All we had to do now was learn how to build one.

At Britannia Heritage Shipyards on the Fraser River, we met Clyde Westman, a veteran seaman. Clyde had a wealth of knowledge about wooden boat building which he was happy to share. That was fortunate because although we'd found many old photographs of scows, we hadn't been able to turn up any hundred-year-old boat-building instructions. All our plans so far were based on hunches.

"I don't think I'd use oakum," he said after I mentioned that I had seen it on most Klondike supply lists. "For the size of boat you're talking about, I'd stuff the cracks with cotton then seal them up with pitch."

"Most Klondikers wouldn't have had such materials," he mused. "They might have just put canvas in the cracks and sealed them with pine pitch."

He told us a story to make his point. "I remember the first boat I built when I was a boy. I borrowed a cotton dress and tore it into strips to place between the planks before sealing them. That boat didn't leak for a whole fishing season—and my mother never did learn what happened to her dress!"

We listened intently as he described the special tamping tools and the cotton we would need. Sally jotted notes as he reviewed our list of supplies for boat building.

As it turned out, our visit to the shipyard was well timed. Clyde was in the middle of a boat restoration project, and offered to let us learn on the job.

"Next week we'll be ready to do the caulking with cotton on this boat," he said. "Why don't you come back then?"

Before we left, Clyde pointed to a scow that lay partially submerged in the river. "I'll teach you to seal your boat right, so it won't end up like that one," he said, chuckling.

When we returned a few days later, Clyde introduced us to everyone in the coffee room. "Ian and Sally are going to build a scow and float down the Yukon River," he said, with such complete assurance that he even had me convinced we could do it. Over coffee, eight experienced boat-builders gave us pointers, not one of them commenting on our lack of experience. We were inspired by their confidence.

The rebuilt boat was ready for caulking. Clyde climbed onto a scaffolding so he could work on the uppermost seam, then began pulling cotton from a bale at his feet. It looked much like cotton wool, but came out in one long strand, two fingers thick. Using a chisel-like tool called a caulking iron, he pushed the cotton into the crack and whacked the iron with a wooden mallet. Clyde collected another length of cotton, stuffed it into the seam with the iron, then swung the mallet again.

"After a while, you'll learn how much cotton is just right," he assured us. Loops of cotton poked out in tufts along the seam. After working down the length of a board, he returned to his starting point. Clyde whacked the caulking iron with the mallet to force each loop of cotton into the crack.

We learned that this cotton was packed in so tightly that if the tiniest bit of water entered the crack, the cotton would expand so that no water could pass through. The principle was so simple. In a few months we would find out for ourselves if it actually worked.

"Can I try?" Sally called up to Clyde. He handed her the caulking iron and mallet.

Sally looked reasonably proficient until she went back to hammer the loops into the crack. Even after pounding the cotton in a second time, there was still a great deal of the caulking that was not in the crack.

"Most people hit too softly," Clyde offered encouragingly as he once again demonstrated the proper technique.

After Sally had completed a board, I climbed the scaffolding to take my turn. My nostrils filled with the pungent, unfamiliar combined aroma of linseed oil, wet cedar, and salt air. The building reverberated with the sounds from hammers, handsaws, and hand planes. As I pounded with the wooden mallet, I had the feeling that the sights and sounds here weren't much different from those of a century ago.

By the time Sally finished hammering cotton along the length of another board, we felt that we had a firm grasp on the theory of caulking. With all our new skills, Sally and I now felt ready to begin our Klondike expedition. Learning how to pan for gold could wait until we arrived in Dawson City.

We began loading our gear into a van we'd rescued from a scrapyard for the drive to Smithers. To spruce up the lopsided, rust-etched van, we had glued a pair of green plastic horns to the hood. A green sign stencilled on the back windows identified our outfit as the "Two Greenhorns Ranch."

In went the pack-boxes, saddles, saddle blankets, ropes, and other horse-related gear. Boxes of clothes, food, and camera equipment were jammed into the remaining spaces. We had already shipped several boxes to Whitehorse, containing the tools to build our scow, as well as the supplies for the rest of our journey. We would pick them up when we got there.

By the morning of May 28, Sally and I were ready for the journey north. The starter turned over reluctantly, but the engine wheezed to life with a satisfying clatter. We were off! As I wrestled with the steering, I hoped the two hundred horses under the hood would get us to Smithers. Then, we could trade the beast for a team of more responsive horses and begin our journey into the past.

Sally leaned out the window as we rolled onto the freeway.

"Klondike Ho!" she shouted, echoing the call of gold-seekers from a hundred years earlier.

THREE

Four Trusty Steeds

As we pulled into the Collingwood's Sometime Never Ranch in Smithers, a denim-clad cowboy tipped his hat to greet us. He was thin as a beanpole, all sinew and muscle. His dusty cowboy hat looked like it had been recently stomped by a bucking bronco.

"That *has* to be Slim," Sally observed as we rattled to a stop.

Slim took a long look at the plastic green horns sprouting from the hood of our van. As he wandered over to meet us, he must have wondered what he was getting into.

Over coffee we chatted with Slim about our upcoming trip. Although Sally and I had learned some basics of working with horses, we knew that we still had much to learn. To our relief, Slim had agreed to give us a crash course in back-country riding, packing, and trail life. We were eager to get started.

"Well, let's go catch your hay-burners. I've found the three I told you about and I have a lead on another one," Slim said, handing me a rope halter. I turned the loop of rope over in my hands and tried to remember how it went on the horse.

As Sally and I walked with Slim towards the field, I noted that he was all cowboy, from his trail-worn Stetson to his western-style shirt, faded jeans, and cowboy boots. I'm sure even the horses were impressed. Here I was in my new hiking boots, unfaded jeans, clean plaid shirt, and just-off-the-shelf hat. I was sure the horses would be able to tell I was a greenhorn.

The first horse to greet us when we leaned over the fence was a big chestnut pot-bellied mare named, of all things, Mare. She studied us with large dark eyes and sniffed our scent, nickering softly.

The next creature that wandered up looked almost identical to Mare. Even though he was slightly smaller, the only way I could tell the two apart was by the blaze of white down Dusty's face.

Finally, a sinewy, black gelding, who pranced and snorted nervously, edged towards us.

"He doesn't have a name," Slim informed us. "He's just called The Black One." Was it just my imagination, or did that sound rather ominous? I looked over at Sally, but she was gazing raptly at the horses.

"Let's call him Blackie," Sally said, sounding smitten.

We were pleased that they all looked well cared for. What a contrast to the horses that many stampeders had started with! Back in 1897, Tappan Adney wrote: "Many horses, alleged to be pack horses . . . had ribs like the sides of a whiskey-cask and hips to hang hats on. Why some look as if a good feed of oats would make them sag beyond remedy." I looked closer at our steeds. None of them resembled Adney's description.

"Where would you like to start?" Slim asked as Sally fed Mare the last of our carrots.

"I think we should try to find another horse," I suggested. We hoped to be on the trail by mid-June, less than two weeks away and we definitely needed at least one more horse to complete our pack string.

We spent the afternoon with Slim taking us from stable to stable as we searched for another horse. Unfortunately,

Slim's leads didn't pan out. Our search the next day brought no better results—no one wanted to sell a horse this close to the summer riding season.

"We'll keep asking around. I'm sure we'll find something," Slim said, trying to soften the blow.

That evening Sally and I visited our horses again. First we caught Dusty. He was a solid-looking animal that stood some fifteen hands high. Slim had told us that he came from a family of large, gentle packhorses, a mix of draft and quarter horse.

"I think he likes me," Sally murmured, feeding Dusty a handful of oats.

"And I think he'd like anyone with a supply of oats," I countered, chuckling as Dusty nuzzled Sally's pocket where she kept a supply of grain.

Next we rounded up Mare. I hadn't realized how tall she was until I started brushing her and had to stand on my toes to reach the top of her mane. Mare's shoulders, the withers, almost came to the top of my head. It would be a challenge to heave a heavy box up onto her back! I looked at Mare's plate-sized hoofs and vowed to keep my own feet away from hers.

Then Sally tried to catch Blackie. He was a high-spirited horse and trotted round and round the paddock with Sally in pursuit. Out of breath, Sally eventually joined Dusty, Mare, and me at the gate and waited. Blackie sidled closer and finally joined us. Ever so slowly, Sally tried to slip a halter onto Blackie. With each slight movement he flinched.

We tried a new approach. Without trying to catch him, Sally started brushing Blackie's mane. He stood swishing his tail nervously as she brushed his thin coat and checked his feet. Then, with one quick motion, she put the halter on.

Sally led Blackie to the fence. He was a slim, fine-boned horse, only slightly taller than a pony, with his withers just reaching Sally's shoulders. Blackie was not the stout mountain horse we'd hoped for, although Slim assured us he would be a good trail horse due to his quarter-horse blood.

"Now that we have horses, I feel as though the trip has finally started," Sally said, swinging the paddock gate closed behind us. While we stood watching our horses, Sally slipped her hand into mine and gave a reassuring squeeze. Both of us knew there was a lot to accomplish in a short time. Even so, we shared the feeling that together we could tackle the challenges that lay ahead.

The next morning we set to work with Slim to practise saddling the horses. While Slim watched, Sally put her saddle on Blackie. No sooner had she tightened the cinch when Blackie started jumping and kicking and lunging and snorting. I stared in awe. To my uninitiated eye, he looked more like a bucking bronco than a saddle horse.

"Guess he's a cold-back," Slim observed when Blackie had calmed down somewhat.

"What's that?" I asked.

"Well, he doesn't like to have a saddle put on."

Great, I thought, a bucking bronco who doesn't like saddles.

"I think the other two are a bit calmer," Slim declared. "Let's practise loading the packsaddles on them." He felt that because Mare and Dusty were large horses, they would be best suited as pack animals.

Not knowing what to expect from Dusty, I cautiously placed a thick felt pad on his back. Next came a metal and wood packsaddle to support the boxes. Sally sorted out a tangle of new cinches, webbing, and miles of leather straps, then passed me the breast collar to clip around Dusty's chest. This would prevent the saddle from sliding back.

"Now lift up his tail and slide the breeching under there— gently," Slim said. "That'll keep the saddle from sliding forward."

When Slim was satisfied with the fit, we hooked the two boxes to the packsaddle and tied them securely. Sally started to put a canvas tarp over the whole load. She had trouble reaching high enough and resorted to throwing the tarp over the top.

With a loud snort, Dusty hopped sideways.

"Ah, the old flying tarp trick!" Slim said. "Works every time!" We were beginning to appreciate his dry sense of humour.

"Try this way," Slim suggested. Slim stood with his shoulder touching Dusty's and held the tarp, which he had folded in four. Nonchalantly, he flopped it onto Dusty's back. "By blocking his view with your body, he won't panic at the sight of this 'thing' coming at him."

Next came the diamond, the final roping to tie everything onto the horse. Slim passed the rope to me. It was time to show our stuff.

Slim was a good instructor, critical of anything not quite right that would affect the horses. As we packed the horse he had patiently pointed out corrections. A cinch, pad, breast collar, or breeching secured in the wrong position would cause a blister or would "sore up" the horse, as Slim put it.

"Most wranglers up here use the single diamond, but that sure looks pretty," Slim observed when we were finished our double diamond.

We stood at Dusty's side waiting for Slim's comments. This time, the saddle was too far forward and we learned that over a long day it would bruise Dusty's withers. Slim ran his fingers under the cinch.

"It's loose," he announced.

"How did that happen?" I asked. Dusty had tricked us. I'd forgotten that he would have taken a deep breath to expand his chest as we prepared to tighten the cinch. I could easily put a span of four fingers between the cinch and Dusty's side. It should have been snug.

Next was the diamond. It had seemed tight enough, but when Slim pulled on the rope it didn't snap sharply against the box as it should have. We needed more practice.

"Let's take a break from this and go for a ride," Slim suggested.

"I'll try Dusty," I offered quickly. No way was I going to get on Blackie. Luckily, Sally thought she would do fine with him.

Slim suggested we load the riding saddles with items we would use during the day. At the back of our saddles, and secured with leather thongs, we put our full-length rain slickers. Sally and I each tied an axe at the front of our saddles under our knees. I was sceptical when Slim insisted we'd become used to the bulge.

"Anyway you'll have to get used to it. Your knees will just change shape!" he said. In addition to the axe under one knee, I had our shotgun secured under the other. As I mounted, I swung my right leg high to clear the bulky saddle.

Perched uncomfortably in the saddle, I looked over to see how Sally was doing. Blackie was not happy. His ears were back and his neck muscles tensed as Sally finished saddling him. I watched with suspense when Sally gave the cinch a final tug.

"I think he's getting used . . ." Sally's sentence was cut short as Blackie suddenly transformed into a bucking bronco.

Sally leaped out of the way, leaving Slim holding the lead line. As if this was normal behavior for a horse, Slim turned in one spot letting Blackie race around the full length of the line. What a performance! Blackie leaped into the air, kicking his rear feet up until he was almost doing a head-stand. I grew dizzy watching him.

"He's ready now," Slim said a few minutes later when Blackie had calmed down. Slim explained that, at eighteen years of age, Blackie had probably developed many bad habits that would be difficult to correct. With some hesitation, Sally swung into the saddle.

Following Slim, we set off through the forest. From our rides in Vancouver, we had expected to be fairly comfortable on the trail but Slim had many surprises for us. He planned to train us for bush riding, not trail riding. After only ten minutes in the saddle, I found myself looking straight down what appeared to be a near-vertical slope.

As I started down, I was sure I'd slide out of the saddle, down Dusty's neck and over his head.

"Make sure you lean back, putting your weight in the stirrups," he called over his shoulder to us. Slim was already halfway to the bottom.

For two hours Slim led us through a thick forest, then on a cross-country jaunt across swamps, through dense brush, and down more steep hills.

"Didn't notice much trail on that trail ride, Slim," I said when we finally returned to the ranch.

"Just showing you the kind of country you'll be travelling through," he replied. Until now, Sally and I hadn't grasped the scope of what we were getting into.

I dismounted stiffly. Every joint in my lower body ached. Now I knew for certain why cowboys were bow-legged. It came from straddling a bulky saddle, two thick saddle pads and a steed as large around as a whisky barrel.

Slim looked at me and smiled knowingly as I rubbed my sore knees. "If you put too much weight in the stirrups, your knees will be sore. If you ride with too much weight in the saddle, your butt will be sore. When your weight is balanced just right, your knees and butt should be equally sore."

The next day Sally and I set off on a ride by ourselves. As we returned through the farmyard, Reg Collingwood came by to see how we were doing. We took the opportunity to ask if he would consider selling us Outlaw, a horse Slim had mentioned as a possible candidate to complete our pack string.

"I'll have to think about it. She's our best wrangle pony," he said, tilting his hat back and rubbing his forehead. Meanwhile, Sally and I would continue phoning other ranches to see if we could round up another horse.

After three days of riding, Slim suggested it was time to lead a packhorse. He gave us a few tips, then handed Sally Mare's lead line.

"Don't ever wrap the lead line around your hand," Slim cautioned. "And remember to look back now and then to see how Mare is doing."

With one hand holding the rope attached to Mare's halter and the other hand holding Blackie's reins, Sally looked pretty busy. I followed on Dusty, keeping my distance.

All went well at first, with Mare obediently following at the end of the lead line. She walked on the right side of Blackie with her nose near his flank. However, as soon as we entered the forest, Blackie went one way around a tree and Mare the other. From my vantage point, I could see what was coming next—as the rope to Mare snubbed around the tree, Sally was jerked back in the saddle.

Sally spun around to see what had happened. True to his nature, Blackie pranced about, but Sally managed to control him with the reins in one hand while coaxing Mare around the tree with the lead rope in the other. After a short tug of war, they continued down the trail.

Twenty paces later the trail passed between two trees. Mare paused for a moment, then rushed through the narrow gap. There was a terrific crash of pack-boxes smashing against tree trunks. Mare flew backwards, yanking the rope from Sally's gloved hand.

"Your turn to lead," Sally said, nursing her sore elbow. I let out my breath, not realizing that I'd been holding it during the commotion. Feeling less than confident after having watched Sally, I dismounted to catch Mare.

I was dismayed to discover how many details there were to pay attention to. I had to guide my horse, choose a route, lead the packhorse, duck under branches, and look over my shoulder frequently to check on Mare's progress. I didn't even have time to pull my prized cowboy hat down before it blew off and landed in the mud. So much for the vision I'd had in the library of passively sitting astride my steed on a mountain trail!

For the rest of our ride it was amusing to watch Mare deal with narrow places in the trail. Each time, she paused to study the gap. I could almost feel her taking a deep breath before rushing ahead to get it over with. I learned to pause at each tight spot to allow Mare time to study the gap then walk through.

Sally took another turn at leading. Feeling more confident, she led Mare through a swamp then across a creek. Over the next couple of hours, we learned to anticipate narrow

Outlaw

Dusty

Blackie

Mare

places in the trail and to avoid low-hanging branches and other hazards.

"Not bad for our first day with a pack string," Sally said as we rode side by side to the farmyard. Reg Collingwood met us again as we rode in.

"Your equipment doesn't look so shiny-new anymore," he observed. "You're starting to look the part." I glanced back at Mare. The rigging was mud-splattered, the diamond rope and the tarp had been scuffed by trees, and the rear breeching was dripping with horse dung. Sally and I looked a little scuffed and mud-splattered as well.

"I've been thinking about Outlaw. She's a bit small for most of my riders, and she is slowing down a bit as a wrangle-pony. I guess I could part with her," Reg said.

Sally let out a whoop and Blackie almost ran Reg over in the excitement.

After unsaddling our horses, we went to meet the newest member of our pack string. Outlaw was a stocky, barrel-sided pony with a shaggy, brown coat. As she walked towards us, she peered placidly through a forelock of long black hair.

"She'd be a good riding horse for Sally," Reg suggested. Reg felt that Outlaw was too small to carry my weight on a long journey.

Although we now had a full string of horses, Sally and I weren't quite ready for the trail. We needed to spend more time in the saddle to get our riding muscles in shape. The horses also needed to build endurance for the strenuous journey ahead.

Between trail rides, Sally and I practised loading the packhorses. One day we timed ourselves. When we had first started, it had taken more than an hour to pack a horse. Now it took only twenty-six minutes. Slim was working with a colt nearby and we asked him to check our work.

"The boxes look about even," he said. He walked to one side and checked the cinch.

"Feels pretty tight," he granted. I flashed a smile to Sally. Then Slim took several steps to the side and looked at the load. He tilted his hat back, rubbed his chin and smiled a crooked smile.

"But the saddle is too far back," Slim said.

Sally and I looked at each other and groaned. It took only a few minutes to untie the diamond hitch, remove the tarp, undo the box rope, remove the boxes, and loosen the cinches. Then we reloaded the whole works. Mare, as patient as ever, stood quietly through the entire process.

We called Slim back again. He squatted to eyeball the boxes, not making any comments this time. Good, I thought, they were even. Next, he studied the boxes from one side then the other, checking to see that each was straight to the horse. Still not saying anything, he ran his fingers under the padding at the withers. He studied the breeching, the breast collar, and the cinches. Finally, he pulled on the diamond rope. It snapped sharply against the box.

"That load won't come loose. It'll hold all day," was his encouraging report.

"Great! Now all we have to do is repeat that every morning for five weeks on the trail," I said to Sally.

Sally and I were pleased with our progress. The only nagging problem was that Blackie was not working out as a saddle horse. He still bucked when first saddled. It was impossible to hold him back going down hills, and he lunged over obstacles rather than taking things slowly. This made it difficult for Mare to follow him. I asked if we could try Blackie as a packhorse instead.

The next morning, Slim gently placed a large felt pad on Blackie's back. Blackie tensed, nose flaring. His tail swished back and forth as Slim sashayed up with the packsaddle and placed it gently onto the pad. Ever so slowly, Slim tightened the front and rear cinches, and buckled on the breast collar.

"I think we'll leave the breeching off for today," Slim said, wiping his brow. I could see the wisdom in not putting the leather strap under Blackie's tail.

Blackie stood stiff-legged as I gently hooked one box,

Ian with Blackie and Mare

Sally with Outlaw and Dusty

then the other on the saddle. His ears went back when I ever so carefully added the tarp. The whites of his eyes showed as Sally and I tied a diamond hitch to secure the boxes.

"Okay, just walk him for a bit," Slim said. He handed Sally the lead rope.

Sally took one step forward and Blackie lit up as if he had firecrackers under the packsaddle. If I had been at a rodeo, I would have admired the arched-backed, champion bucking-horse style of our black beast. If I had been at a rodeo, I would have cheered loudly as Sally scrambled to keep out of the way of the wild horse. But I wasn't merely a spectator. I was about to spend two months in close contact with this crazed creature.

"I don't think he likes pack-boxes," Slim observed as we looked on from a safe distance. I was sure Sally had arrived at the same conclusion. The boxes rattled like castanets as the contents inside were tossed about. Luckily the diamond hitch remained tight and the boxes stayed on.

Finally, Sally realized that she should lunge Blackie as Slim had done. She stood in one place, letting him buck and kick in a circle around her. After a few minutes of this, he tired of the game and calmed down.

"That was quite a performance, but at least you didn't have a wreck," Slim said.

"What's that?"

"You have a wreck when a loaded packhorse crashes into something and the boxes come off, burst open, and the contents get stomped into the mud."

I pondered the implications of such an event, and it was now apparent why Blackie had been sold by his previous owner. He was an uncooperative saddle horse and didn't take kindly to being a packhorse. That didn't make him good for much.

"I think he'll be okay as a riding horse. He just needs a little work," Slim said, sensing our disappointment. Blackie would have to work out—we had been unable to find any other horses.

Then I realized what that meant. *I* would have to ride The Black One. Slim's words of encouragement did little to ease my horror at having to use Blackie for my saddle horse.

Sally and I took the horses on longer rides each day. As Slim had predicted, the horses gradually became calmer and more cooperative. Even Blackie started to show signs of becoming a reasonably good saddle horse. His delusion that he was a rodeo star seemed to be fading.

"Well, I think you're about as ready as you will ever be," Slim said when we returned from a ride one afternoon. "The rest you'll have to learn on the trail."

I looked back to Sally and grinned. This day had been our fastest saddling and packing so far. The saddle cinches had remained snug, the pack-boxes were still sitting square, and we had ridden for five hours without any mishaps.

With our apprenticeship completed, Sally and I made arrangements with a local farmer to transport us, the horses, and all our gear north to Telegraph Creek. From there, we would start our horseback journey along the Stikine Trail.

The day before leaving, we passed one last test. As we rode along a trail a grouse suddenly burst up from under Outlaw's nose. The bird rushed at the horses, squawking and flapping its wings. I had trouble not laughing when Outlaw leaped sideways, almost leaving Sally behind. Blackie joined in the four-hoofed tap dance, but Sally and I remained securely in our saddles. With a minimum of fuss, we also kept control of the horses we led.

"I think we're ready," Sally said, looking back at me. "But if the past ten days are any indication, our trip to the Klondike will be quite a challenge!"

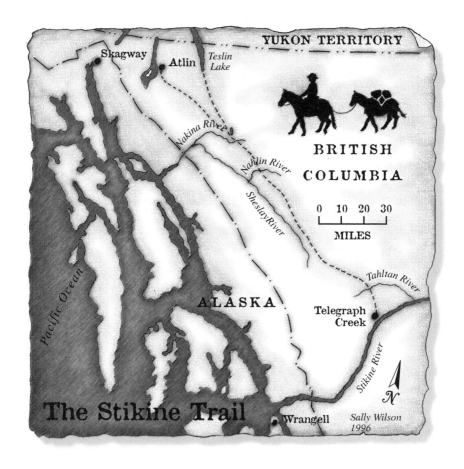

The Stikine Trail

FOUR

North by Packhorse

"Doesn't look like much of a trail," Sally commented as we climbed into our saddles and began riding north.

Ahead was only a narrow, indistinct trail that led from the Stikine River through dense forest. But then, we hadn't expected much. A report from 1898 had stated, "The rough trail leads into the forest only a short way and then disappears into mud, swamp and tangled brush." We hoped that the conditions would be better than they were during the Klondike days.

Even with the knowledge of the trail's difficulties, I felt a strange mixture of calm and excitement. The logistics of planning and packing and the days of learning new skills were behind us. It was June 20 and for the next five weeks our world would consist of four horses, each other, and the wilderness around us.

It was a steady climb from Telegraph Creek in a steady drizzle. Even though the trail was muddy and wet, we were starting to think that it wouldn't be so bad after all. Then we came to a tangle of wind-felled trees blocking the path for as far as we could see.

"I'll chop the first one," I said, sliding off Blackie.

Fortunately, the horses stood quietly and didn't seem to mind the commotion of me hacking at the tree.

Soon I was sweating profusely under my rain slicker. It was hard work chopping the tree with a small axe. With each blow, a slice of wood flew up. Forty chops later the tree finally dropped to the ground. If only we'd brought the bow saw. We had left it behind at the last minute because it was too awkward to pack.

Only twenty paces later, it was Sally's turn to chop through the next tree. This time the tree didn't drop to the ground. Instead, it remained hanging horizontally across the trail, shoulder-high to Sally. I took my turn hacking a second notch. Finally, a section of the log crashed to the ground, leaving a gap just wide enough for the horses.

"I never know if we should mount up or just walk," Sally groaned when we stopped for the tenth time that morning. Wind-felled trees lay in a tangle across the trail and there was rarely a safe route around them. One side of the trail dropped into the roaring Telegraph Creek; the other side was equally steep and criss-crossed with a labyrinth of fallen trees.

Eight hours later, we came to a clearing as the trail topped the hill. At Summit Lakes we unpacked the horses for the night.

"Tough day," Sally said to me over Mare's withers.

My only reply was a tired grunt as I lowered a pack-box to the ground. We had travelled a mere six miles, most of it by hacking our way with axes through blowdown.

After unpacking and unsaddling the horses, we turned them out to feed. But first, we buckled a pair of hobbles onto each horse to prevent our trusty steeds from heading home. While I held each horse, Sally secured the wide leather straps on their front legs just above the hoofs.

In the tent that night, we settled against saddle pads and began writing in our journals. We were trail-weary, but happy that our first day had passed without any "wrecks" or other predicted disasters.

Once in our sleeping bags, we listened to the sounds

around us—the stomping of hoofs, the occasional snort, and the rhythmical clanging of bells as the hobbled horses hopped around the meadow. Then we heard the sound of a horse near our heads.

"Noisy eater," I whispered to Sally. We could clearly hear the slapping of the horse's lips collecting a mouthful of grass, followed by loud chewing noises. *Slap, slap, rip, crunch, crunch.*

Next came a loud snort as the hobbled horse heaved its front legs into the air for a leap forward. It landed with a heavy thump. Moments later, a second snort indicated the animal had just lunged into the air for another step.

Suddenly, the whole tent shook as the four-footed beast tripped on a rope.

"Getoutathere!" I shouted, banging on the tent wall. A clanging bell and the shaking ground confirmed the horse was jumping to another location.

Sally and I slept lightly that night, listening for the reassuring sound of the horses' bells. Blackie and Outlaw were tied to pickets but Dusty and Mare were only restrained with hobbles. We hoped they would stay close to the tent, but not too close. Every time I woke, the tinkling of four bells was music to my ears.

When I peered out of the tent in the morning, I was greeted with the sight of frost on the grass and ice in the water buckets. Summer hadn't arrived yet in the mountains. I counted four horses, breaths steaming in the cold dawn air.

"Looks like a great morning, and the horses are all here," I reported to Sally.

"All right! Let's hit the trail."

After breakfast cooked over a campfire, we packed up and began loading the horses. I placed the saddle pads and packsaddle on Mare, checking that they were positioned properly over her withers. Sally ran her hand under the pad and pulled out a few strands of Mare's mane. Many stampeders hadn't been so careful and books tell sad stories of horses rubbed raw by incorrectly loaded packs. We took our time with each horse, paying attention to all the important details.

Loading Mare

Sally with Dusty

We followed Slim's suggestion of saddling our riding horses before loading the boxes onto the packsaddles. Sure enough, when we returned to Mare she had relaxed and let out her breath, leaving the cinches hanging loosely.

"Tighten them quickly," Sally said, "before she takes a deep breath!"

The boxes felt especially heavy when I lifted them up to the packsaddle. I wondered what Mare thought of having a pair of sixty-five-pound boxes plus a twenty-five-pound top load piled on her back.

I lifted the second pack-box and rested it on my knee to adjust my grip. With a bounce and a shove, I heaved it to the top of the saddle, which was almost eye level. From the other side, Sally grabbed the box rope and hooked it over the bars of the saddle.

As Slim had done, I stood back and eyed the boxes. Yes, they were parallel to Mare's back. I added the top load of duffle bags containing our clothes, stake-out ropes, extra hobbles, and halters.

While Sally held Mare's lead line, I placed a tarp on the load then unfolded the canvas a little at a time. I knew that one gust of wind could turn the tarp into a flapping, horse-startling mass of canvas that would set Mare crow-hopping around the clearing. I didn't need the excitement.

Even after all our days of practice, the double diamond took a lot of time and effort to tie. Once tied, we followed the rope around, pulling it even tighter. I walked around Mare in time to see Sally swinging from the rope as she pulled with all of her weight. Other times she would brace herself, using a knee or shoulder to push against the box.

As usual Mare grunted and groaned in protest.

"Don't you feel guilty when Mare moans like that?" I asked.

"No, she'd complain more if the load slid under her belly!"

Our last task was to load Dusty. In addition to his pair of boxes, Dusty carried the sleeping bags and the bulky rolled-up tent. To remind us of our distant goal, we tied the gold pan in the centre of the diamond on one of his pack-boxes.

"I'm tuckered out and we haven't even hit the trail yet," I said, wiping sweat from my brow. Although we had crawled out of bed at six that morning, it was already ten o'clock.

Before mounting up, I led Blackie and Mare a short distance from Sally's horses. Then I swung into the saddle. This went smoothly except for Mare's lead line, which somehow ended up under my leg.

"Needs practice," Sally said helpfully. Her laughter distracted me as I tried to untangle the rope. Blackie started trotting down the trail.

"Whoa, Blackie," I coaxed, pulling back on the reins. One of Blackie's many bad habits was to start moving before I was ready. Finally I sorted out horses, reins, and lead lines. We were on our way.

It was pleasant riding through an open meadow for the first hour. Then we entered another storm-battered forest. We slowed to a snail's pace, chopping trees as we went.

Several miles later, the trail split. As would happen many times in the weeks to come, we had to guess which of two trails to follow. Both headed in roughly the direction we wanted to go, and both were equally faint. Which one? With fingers crossed, we took the left fork.

We weren't far down our chosen route when the barely discernible trail plunged into thick willows. I looked back and could see only Sally's head and shoulders above the tangle. Outlaw was there somewhere, buried in the bushes. Twisting left and right, we worked our way around deadfalls and branches and bushes. Finally, the faint trail emerged from the willows. It led straight up the side of a mountain.

"Let's take a look at the map again," I suggested when Sally caught up with me. We tied the horses to trees and pulled the map from Sally's saddlebag.

I compared the contours of the map to the hills around us. A quick triangulation with the compass confirmed my hunch. "Guess what? I think we should've taken the other fork," I reported.

"No kidding!" Sally said, looking up the steep mountain in front of us.

We backtracked through the willows, then started on the other trail.

I was just thinking of how well Blackie was behaving, when the rope that led from my right hand to Mare's halter looped underneath Blackie's tail. Now if there's one thing a horse doesn't like it's a rope burn under the tail. Blackie squealed, then lunged forward. Mare's lead line went tight and almost pulled me out of the saddle.

Then I felt the saddle shift under me. With an explosive, arched-back buck, my trusty mount took me towards the sky. Suddenly, I was flying instead of riding. Something told me that the landing would not be as smooth as the take-off.

I was right. When Blackie hit the ground, I landed hard in the saddle, my teeth rattling with the impact. Only my grip on the horn held me in the saddle as Blackie bucked and kicked and lunged. It was poor style for a rodeo, but there was no judge, no ten-second clock, and no cheering crowd.

On the second buck, my hat flew off and Blackie whirled and stomped it into the mud with his steel-shod forefeet. I could only be glad my head wasn't in the hat at the time.

Finally, the rope fell out from under his tail and he calmed down. Keeping my left hand firmly on the horn, I slowly swung out of the saddle. I picked up my jumped-on hat and stood there, trembling and glaring at Blackie.

"I think The Black One is a good name after all."

"And I think this would be a good place to call it a day," Sally said, bravely suppressing her laughter. I looked around, and mentally ticked off the requirements for a good camp: water, a meadow with grass, and trees to tie the horses to. At least Blackie had chosen a good spot to act up.

That evening, sitting around the campfire, we thought about the gold-seekers who had been on the trail a century ago. We felt a kinship with them. Although we were not related to them, somehow Sally and I felt that the Klondikers were our ancestors in a more important way: with their sense of adventure, daring, and risk taking, they were a kind of lifestyle-grandparents for us. They knew what it was to assess the pitch of a mountain trail, to ford a rushing river, to sip pine needles in tea.

If we had accompanied the Klondikers in the days of the gold rush, we would have shared our campsite with dozens of other travellers. More than three thousand had attempted the Stikine Trail, lured this way by the false promise of a wagon road and the fact that they would avoid paying American duty on their outfits. Although we were making our journey long after the stampeders, we often thought of the people we had seen in old photographs. Their familiar faces came to us sometimes in the campfire smoke or shadows. Old Iron Grip would have enjoyed my rodeo with Blackie today, I thought, chuckling to myself. He even might have dropped the shovel he was gripping so tightly.

The next days brought more willows and an indistinct trail littered with fallen trees. Again and again, we had to chop through trees or detour through thick brush. In other places the trail was barely wide enough for the packhorses to squeeze between the trees. Dusty appeared to know the exact width of his load, although a long crease in the gold pan was a reminder of one spot that proved to be a bit too narrow. Mare still rushed through tight spots, often spooking Blackie as she clattered up behind us.

One evening, after searching in vain for a place to pitch our tent, we were forced to camp in the middle of the trail. It was a tiny opening in a forest of willows—the first clearing we'd seen all day. Although there was little feed for the horses, it was too late to continue travelling. Everyone was tired.

"This'll have to do," Sally said with a sigh. "It isn't very good but I can't go farther." We had been on the trail for eleven hours.

It was after midnight when we finally crawled into our sleeping bags. We lay listening to Mare and Dusty. They were hobbled and stomped heavily past the tent. Outlaw and Blackie were tethered to trees; there had been no room to stake them out and there was not much for them to eat anyway.

"Can you hear the bells?" I asked, elbowing Sally a short time later.

"No," came her mumbled reply, "but they won't have left the others. They must be resting." She buried her head in the sleeping bag.

Minutes passed and I heard nothing except birds and mosquitoes.

"Do you think they've gone?" I prodded again. Blackie answered my question with a loud, raspy neigh.

"They *have* gone!" I shouted, leaping out of the bag.

This was every packer's nightmare! In the half-light of the northern night, Sally and I hurriedly pulled on pants and boots. We each grabbed a halter as we burst out of the tent.

After racing down the trail for a few minutes, I stopped and put an arm up to prevent Sally from crashing into me.

"Listen!"

"I can't hear anything over my breathing," she said between gasps.

From far ahead I heard the faint tinkle of a bell. A few minutes of jogging brought the horses in sight. Unfortunately, they saw us at the same time.

"They're running away!" I said, surprised. For some reason, I had thought they would be glad to see us.

The chase was on! Despite being restricted by hobbles, they easily negotiated thick bushes, fallen trees, and boulders.

"Cut them off!" Sally yelled when they veered towards the trail. With a desperate lunge I grabbed Mare's mane.

"So, you're the troublemaker," I said accusingly, slipping on a halter.

Back in camp Sally said, "If we tie Mare, I don't think Dusty would leave on his own."

An hour later the alarm rang, jolting us out of a deep sleep. It was Sally's turn to check on the horses at three o'clock in the morning. As she dragged herself out of bed, her only comment was, "I read that wranglers don't get much sleep. I guess the book was right."

"It's lucky I have a large bladder and don't have to get up," came my sympathetic reply.

By mid-morning the next day, we reached the Tahltan River. During the gold rush, the process of relaying a year's supply of gear was so time-consuming that many of the gold-seekers who set off in August had only reached the Tahltan River by the middle of October. By then, deep snow hindered their progress. The distance from Telegraph Creek was only forty miles and had taken us five days, but many Klondikers had travelled back and forth over the rough trail a dozen or more times.

Many people hadn't come even this far. Disgusted by the condition of the trail, they had turned around and taken the paddlewheelers back down the Stikine River to the coast. Some went home, but most went on to try other routes to the gold-fields.

I looked around the clearing for signs of old cabins, but only a few foundation logs remained. Here at the Tahltan River, a number of the thwarted Klondikers had built log cabins to den up for the cold months ahead. Packhorses that would have slowly starved to death through the winter had been mercifully shot. In late winter, the stampeders continued their journey by snowshoe and sled.

Not long after reaching the river, we climbed into more open country. I rode, lost in thought, watching the horses weave through the aspen forest. Sally and I didn't talk much on the trail. To do so, we would have had to yell because our horses were usually far apart. We preferred the solitude of the trail and shared our impressions of the day each time we stopped to rest.

It felt magical riding through the aspens. The creamy-white trunks stretched skyward, then formed a sheltering canopy of green. The forest floor was a knee-high carpet of blue lupines in full bloom. This was what we had hoped for on this trip, and I certainly didn't miss trail clearing.

Late that afternoon we came to a meadow with new grass, just beginning to turn green. We stopped for the night, happy that the horses could have a reasonably good feed at last.

"This place is called Saloon," Sally told me as she checked

Our pack string heading north

Camp chores

the map. Few landmarks were named, so we guessed that this had been a stopping place during the gold rush as well.

After unpacking and unsaddling the horses, we hobbled them and turned them out to feed. By our second night, we had discovered that Blackie couldn't be hobbled. He had fought the leather straps, tugging first with his left foot then the right until his fetlocks were nearly raw. There was no choice but to picket him each night. I drove a stake into the centre of a clearing and secured one end of a long rope to it. The other end I tied to one of Blackie's front legs.

Sally and I kept watch on the horses while they grazed. We had already seen how fast they could canter when hobbled, and we had no energy left for a high-speed chase. Mare was an accomplished hurdler when wearing hobbles. It was amusing to watch her swing her front feet high into the air as though clearing some large obstacle each time she moved.

"They must be hungry," I said. "Usually they roll first." This early in the season, grass was sparse and the horses had found little to eat along the way.

Blackie was the first to take a break from eating and start to roll. He selected a spot by sniffing the ground and testing its firmness by pawing. When he found the perfect spot, Blackie dropped to his front knees and smoothly lowered himself to the ground. After a couple of energetic swings, he rolled onto his back where he wiggled and squirmed, kicking his feet in the air.

"That looks like ecstasy," Sally said, absent-mindedly scratching her back. We watched as Blackie worked sand into the itchy spots he couldn't reach any other way.

"I bet that feels nice," she added. I still didn't get the hint.

"Hey! Would you scratch my back please? Or do I have to roll?"

While I scratched Sally's back, the other horses followed Blackie's example. We'd already noticed that they often copied each other's actions. One after the other, the horses wriggled about until they were plastered with dust. In turn, each horse rolled and grunted and snorted, then stood up and gave a vigorous shake.

Not wanting a repeat of the previous night's chase, we put Mare and Outlaw on pickets when we were ready to turn in for the night. Working together, Sally and I hacked at the willows with axes until two more stake-out areas were clear of any obstacles that might snag a picket rope or injure a horse. Then we cut two wooden stakes and drove them deep into the ground. Only Dusty was hobbled and left free to roam.

After watering the horses, Sally and I dived into the tent to escape zillions of black flies. The wind had stilled and almost immediately the flies had appeared. The cloud of bugs was so thick we could hardly see the horses through the screened tent door.

Mare stomped her feet every few seconds and spent the rest of the time rubbing her chest and front legs with her chin. Blackie shook his head constantly, and Dusty had disappeared into a clump of willows. Only Outlaw kept eating, enduring the bugs.

Among our horse-care supplies, we had one small tin of insect repellant for bad days. This looked like a bad day. After pouring a capful of the lemon-scented oil onto a rag, I wiped it on the most tender parts of each horse. They would have to use their tails to swish away the rest of the bugs. This citronella would be more efficient than the smoky fires that Klondikers had kept burning through the night to keep mosquitoes and black flies away.

It was ten o'clock by the time we had completed our chores. There was certainly no sleeping pill like a long day outdoors, and we fell asleep as soon as our heads hit the makeshift pillows of stuff sacks filled with clothing.

While Sally packed up camp the next morning, I scouted the trail ahead.

"The trail seems to cross the Little Tahltan River," I reported on my return, "and the river looks high. All I could see on the other side was a wall of willows."

"This is one of the places where the trail is missing on the map. Maybe it goes along the creek bed," Sally said.

"Well, it might in mid-July when the water is low. But not

now. You'd better come with me to see for yourself."

We spent the entire day clearing a trail through the willows and scouting a route along the hillside. However, when we came to a landslide it became obvious we had no choice but to enter the Little Tahltan River.

We walked down to the river bank and pushed aside the willows so we could see farther up the river.

"We could ride up this side as far as the gravel bar," Sally suggested. "Then we could cross to that sandbar." That was as far as we could see.

"I guess we'll have to choose the rest of our route when we get there," I decided, peering over Sally's shoulder.

Back at camp the horses were standing quietly where we had tied them to trees. We had tied Mare's rope with a double hitch, having learned of her ability to work knots loose with her lips. Double knots were beyond her Houdini-like abilities. Dusty was still at his tree, although the tree was now lying on the ground. He had developed a habit of pulling back against trees, and true to his nature he had felled the aspen we had tied him to.

It was already late, so we decided not to move on. After turning the horses out to graze, Sally and I made adjustments to our outfit and repaired torn saddlebags.

That night I didn't sleep well. I dreamed that I was being washed down the river. The water was deep and the current was swift. In vivid, full-colour detail, Blackie lost his footing on the round boulders and we both plunged into the icy water. My nightmare probably had been initiated by the stories we'd been told about the dangers of crossing rivers this early in the season. Many people had warned us that the water would be too high.

Sally woke first the next morning.

"Time to get up. Today we cross our first river!" she said, leaping out of bed.

"Mmmm, great," I mumbled, trying to shake the night's images from my mind. By the time my first mug of coffee was empty, the mental pictures had faded. Another mug and I was ready to tackle the new day.

FIVE

On the Trail

"Hee-yaaa!" Sally shouted, urging Outlaw on. As they stepped into the river, water splashed up in a spray of glistening drops. We had decided that Outlaw should lead because she was always calm and cool. We hoped that Blackie and the others would follow her example.

I could feel Blackie tense under me as he worked his way down to the river. At the river's edge he froze and stared at the water.

"Go, Blackie! Hee-yaaa!" I goaded him onward, kicking his sides with my heels.

With each step we took, the river became deeper. Water surged against Blackie's chest. He worked hard, fighting the current as we crossed and recrossed the river from gravel bar to gravel bar.

"It's easy for you," Sally yelled over the roar of the current as Outlaw stepped into the water again. "Outlaw is so short the water sprays up and we both get soaked!" They looked very small as they struggled across the river, whitewater foaming around them.

Fortunately, the horses knew what to do and everyone stayed calm. Even when we made the horses walk across stretches of round, football-sized rocks in the river, they took their time and carefully chose their footing.

An occasional cowboy-style whoop from us kept the horses moving. After winding back and forth across the river several times, we found a trail leading up the valley.

"We made it!" I cheered. Sally laughed when I told her of my nightmare from the night before.

"I had the same thoughts," she confided. Our first river crossing hadn't been nearly as difficult as we had feared. We hoped that we would have the confidence and skills necessary to cross the big rivers farther north by the time we reached them.

For the rest of the day, the trail was relatively easy to follow. It disappeared now and then across boggy stretches, but we were able to find it again at the other side of each swamp. In one stretch of wet ground, we found a series of small logs that had been laid side by side to span the bog. This was one of many "corduroy" sections that had been constructed along the route.

The logs had rotted and our horses had a difficult time picking their way over the corduroy. Gingerly, Blackie took a step, feeling under the surface of the dark water for something solid to put his weight on. He took another step. Then, with a great splash he slipped off the log. The log tipped up and one end surged out of the water, like a dark menacing creature from the depths.

In a state of panic, Blackie lunged ahead.

"Easy, Blackie," I said in as calm a voice as I could muster. I knew that if he got a foot stuck between two logs we'd be in serious trouble. With tight reins, I struggled to hold him back until we were through. Luckily, we didn't come to any more stretches of corduroy for the rest of the day.

"Maybe those who had started late in the season had the right idea, after all," I mused that evening. "Then all the swamps would have been frozen."

When we woke the morning of June 26, it looked as though the swamps could still freeze, after all. The meadow was white with frost, and once again there was ice on the

A river crossing

Camp life

water buckets. On cold mornings like this, I enjoyed the morning ritual of lighting the campfire. As a Klondiker might have done years ago, I snapped off dry under-branches from a spruce tree, then gathered an armful of dead wood. As I coaxed the flames to life and added larger pieces of wood, I savoured the fire's warmth and the aroma of wood smoke.

I tossed a handful of coffee grounds into a pot filled with water from the creek and hung the pot over the flames. It wasn't long before wisps of steam drifted from under the lid. Ah, coffee! I plucked the pot from the flames with a bandanna-wrapped hand and filled two enamel mugs.

While the oatmeal bubbled, Sally organized our lunch for the day and packed it in her saddlebags along with bottles of water. Today it would be bannock that we had baked in the gold pan. For snacks Sally packed some hard candies and a mixture of dried fruit and nuts.

With breakfast finished, we completed packing. I stood in front of the four pack-boxes and mentally reviewed which items went in which box. The boxes were identical except for the numbers we had written on each one to tell them apart. Breakfast was in number one, lunch in two and three, supper in number four.

Fuel bottles, pots and pans, horseshoes, and tools were shuffled from box to box to even the weight of each load. We had learned the hard way that we should pad the kitchen supplies to prevent them from rattling and spooking a horse.

I hung one of Dusty's boxes from a scale and noted its weight of sixty pounds. At the start of our trip six days ago, each box had weighed more than sixty-five pounds. The boxes were becoming lighter, and so were the horses, judging by the length of their cinch straps. Sally and I had taken in our belts a notch or two as well. Travelling the old way to the Klondike was hard work!

While I finished packing, Sally caught the horses and tethered them to trees. They knew the routine and waited quietly. In turn, each horse watched Sally stack the appropriate riding tack or pack equipment beside them.

Sally began to brush Dusty, and I watched her pause to run her hand over a lump on his side. Having four horses was like having four children; we worried about each scratch, each scrape. A strange lump had formed just ahead of Dusty's front cinch. Although it was the size of an egg, it moved freely under the skin and didn't appear to bother him.

Each time we stopped that day, Sally checked Dusty to make sure his lump wasn't being rubbed by the cinch.

"Still looks okay," Sally said, turning to me at our lunch break. We had been on the trail for almost four hours and it was lunch time for the horses too. Because there was still little for the horses to eat, we let them graze when we could.

When we found a grassy meadow by an old cabin that evening, Sally and I decided to stop early and make camp. We already knew not to pass up good feed for the horses; the next suitable meadow might be days away.

Once the horses were unpacked, we tended to any rope burns, scrapes, or cuts. I held Blackie's halter while Sally applied a combined insect repellant and antiseptic cream to his lower legs. Blackie was still learning about ropes, and had several rope burns on his fetlocks from becoming tangled in his stake-out line. Dusty's lump didn't seem to be getting any worse, and Outlaw and Mare were problem-free except for a few scratches.

"The horses will be busy grazing for a while," Sally said as we watched our trail companions munching on the grass. "Let's explore the cabin."

We hadn't seen many signs of people along the trail, but then, not many stampeders had made it even this far. The cabin hadn't been used in years, except by small four-footed creatures. Mushrooms lined the shelves where squirrels had carefully stacked them to dry, and the distinct odour of porcupines permeated the room.

Because we had stopped early, Sally and I had time to have a bath in a creek and to do some laundry. We'd been travelling for seven days and our clothes had taken on the essence of life on the trail. Despite daily scrubbing, our hands and fingernails were permanently black with fine dust and sweat from the horses. Everything smelled of horse, from our shirts and chaps to the bottom of our boots. Even the tent smelled of horse. We lessened the aroma by no longer bringing in the damp, horsehair-matted saddle pads to sleep on.

Sally and I spent the evening catching up on chores that we hadn't had time for. Sally's first task was to repair her chaps. When she had jumped off Outlaw a few days ago, the buckle holding her chaps up had caught on the axe handle and torn loose. Splicing a new halter rope and repairing a saddlebag, torn from being snagged on a tree, kept me busy.

To keep away from the hungry black flies, we were working in the tent. It was crowded. Our zipped-together sleeping bags took up most of the space. With day packs, rain gear, clothes bags, camera bags, journals, and many other things that simply had to be in the tent, there was not much room to move.

We left the rain flap open so that we could look through the mosquito netting at the scenery and the horses while we worked on our projects. The horses were content to graze and rest for hours. They dozed while on their feet, and the only sign of life was the occasional swish of a tail to chase away the flies and mosquitoes. When the bugs became worse in a lull of the breeze, the horses stood head to tail, swishing each other's face. Sometimes they stood with their heads and chests stuffed into dense willow bushes for protection from their winged tormentors.

From that camp the trail began to climb the slopes above Kennicott Lake. We were happy to leave the lowland and its swamps—until the trail led us across a steep slope, high above the valley.

"It looks more like a goat path than a horse trail," Sally commented.

I edged my feet out of the stirrups, until only the toes of my boots were perched on the bars. I was ready to bail out at any moment.

I felt Blackie pause, then he carefully chose his next step

as he made his way cautiously across the slope.

"Keep going," I said to Sally when she stopped to admire the view. The tone of urgency in my voice had the desired effect—she pushed Outlaw along. So far I had stolen only quick glances at the sparkling lake below.

Fortunately, for all their shortcomings, our horses were good mountain travellers. Even Blackie was confident. As we worked our way across the last stretch, my feeling of nervousness was replaced by a sense of awe. The horses made their way across the mountainside as sure-footed as mountain goats.

I felt the rhythmical rocking motion of Blackie and listened to the metal shoes of the horses clatter and ring against the rocks. Leaning forward, I adjusted my weight in the saddle to help Blackie step over a boulder straddling the path.

"Way to go, Blackie," I said softly and he turned his ears back to listen to my words of encouragement. I leaned forward and stroked his neck in thanks for the smooth ride.

Late in the afternoon, the trail disappeared into a beaver pond and flooded valley. The only possible route led along a steep-sided slope just above the pond. We checked the map.

"According to the map, there's only a stream here, not a beaver pond," I said. "Hah!" Over the years many features had changed. River banks had collapsed, taking the trail with it, and beaver ponds had flooded valleys, drowning the trail. We could only guess where the trail might be now. Our challenge was to find a way around this latest obstacle.

"I'll go and scout the route," Sally volunteered.

The horses and I remained perched uncomfortably on the hillside while Sally walked ahead.

"It's too steep. I think we should try to go along the edge of the beaver pond," Sally reported on her return. She had found several game paths but each led straight up the hill or petered out at the bluffs.

Having no other choice, we started along the shore of the pond, pushing our way through the brush at the base of the bluff. Now and then, I could just make out a faint trail under the water. Was that the trail we were searching for?

Or was it just the tracks of a moose that had wandered through the pond?

Because of the tangle of willows, we were forced to climb higher and higher. Each horse scrambled for footing on the loose rock. Dusty was only two paces ahead of us when his pack-box hit a tree, dislodging the gold pan. The pan rattled and clanged down the rocky slope, spooking Blackie.

Blackie snorted, did a four-footed tap dance, then lost his footing and started sliding down the hill. In a split second, I rolled out of the saddle on the uphill side and landed hard. Blackie tumbled the other way. I turned in time to see him leap into the water and land with a terrific splash.

Then I realized Mare was about to follow Blackie!

"Whoa, Mare. Whoa," I pleaded. I scrambled down the slope and grabbed her lead line as she was about to plunge into the water. Using what I hoped was a calm-sounding voice, I tried coaxing Blackie to shore. A whinny from Mare was far more effective. At her call, he swam back to join us.

"How do you like my route so far?" Sally asked after she had retrieved her battered gold pan. It was just as well she didn't wait for my reply.

"I think we should go back and cross the creek just before the pond," she said. "When I was up the hill, I saw an aspen grove and a meadow on the other side."

I certainly had no desire to try riding Blackie across the slope again and readily agreed. Sally has a knack of finding trails, so after we crossed the creek I remained with the horses while she scouted for a trail through the forest.

Outlaw perked her ears forward half an hour later, alerting me to Sally's return. It wasn't long before Sally burst into the clearing.

"I walked forever through thick spruce and willow," she said, then paused to catch her breath. "I kept stopping to listen, knowing that eventually I'd hear the aspen leaves rustling in the wind. The meadow is beautiful, and I found a game trail leading right to it!"

The meadow made a perfect campsite. Unfortunately, the next morning brought more challenges. The only way

To the high country

Walking down a steep slope

67

forward was through a flooded forest and across another beaver pond.

Once in the pond, Sally called back to me. "Go slowly. There are sharp sticks poking up everywhere!"

By the time her horses had waded through the pond, the water was so murky I couldn't see the bottom or any of the sticks. As soon as I was out of the water, I inspected the horses' legs. I was relieved that there were no serious cuts.

As we entered an aspen grove, I looked ahead to Sally. She looked so comfortable in the saddle. I smiled when she urged Outlaw on with her heels. Outlaw must have spotted the lush grass at the side of the trail, and by kicking Outlaw on, Sally let her know that she had noticed too. Outlaw couldn't resist though and snatched a mouthful of grass on the move.

"Get up, Piggy," I heard Sally say to her saddle horse. This was a constant game they played. Judging by the size of Outlaw's girth, which hadn't shrunk since we had started on the trail, I'd say Outlaw was winning.

Sally turned in the saddle and glanced over her shoulder at Dusty.

"Come on, Dusty," she called, flicking the lead line between them. Sally held the line loosely in her right hand, resting on her thigh. Dusty was Outlaw's friend and followed at just the right distance with his nose near her right flank. They were a good team.

"The horses are starting to work well together," I said to Sally that afternoon when we stopped for a rest.

"Yeah, sure beats walking. What a wonderful way to travel." Sally smiled and threw her arms around Outlaw's neck. Then she turned and gave me an equally big hug.

The trail led us down a narrow valley, through more wetlands and dense forests. As we wound through the forest, I noticed the trail was punctuated by moose prints and droppings. Now and then I saw wolf droppings as well, but they didn't appear to bother the horses.

Bear scat certainly did. The horses shied away and danced around the area, snorting and breathing heavily, with nostrils flared.

"Easy, easy," I said, running my hand along Blackie's neck. I looked down and saw bear tracks larger than Dusty's size two horseshoe prints.

Fortunately, the bear tracks veered away not long after that. All was well until that night when we were setting pickets for the horses.

"Ian! A bear!" I heard Sally hiss from the other side of a cluster of bushes.

My heartbeat quickened as I scanned the area. At the edge of the forest, right where I had planned to stake one of the horses, was an enormous black bear. My first concern was for the horses. Would they panic and try to run away? With hobbles on, they could not outrun a bear.

The bear was skulking through the woods, circling our camp.

"Get Blackie and Mare out of here," I said in a loud whisper to Sally. They were the most easily spooked horses.

While Sally led the horses away, I banged pots and pans together, hoping to create a frightening and intolerable noise.

The bear didn't even flinch. This was a dangerous animal.

Grabbing the shotgun from our pile of gear, I fired a shot over its head.

"The bear's gone, but I think we should move camp," I said to Sally when I caught up with her. Although it was ten o'clock and we were tired from a long day, this was obviously the bear's territory.

"You're right. We can't stay here," Sally agreed. "We'd be too worried to sleep anyway." Wearily, we reloaded the horses and moved camp. The glamour of trail life was starting to wear a bit thin.

Even though we camped several miles away, we slept lightly. In our imaginations, every rustle of leaves and every snort from a horse meant that the bear had found us.

Sally and I were happy to leave camp in the morning. As we climbed steadily upwards in the heat of the day, the horses continued to amaze us with their stamina. Remembering what Slim had told us, we stopped the sweating horses frequently to let them catch their breaths. The horses nickered softly each time we neared a creek, reminding us to let them have a long drink.

It was pleasantly cooler where the trail twisted upwards through mature groves of balsam poplar, their canopies of green sheltering us from the sun.

For the first time on the trail, we had a view of where we were going and where we'd been. Until now we'd been in valleys, often hemmed in by forests. We had plotted our progress on the maps but had not seen much of the surrounding area. Now we enjoyed the broad perspective. In the distance to the west were snow-covered peaks of the high, cloud-piercing Boundary Range. Directly below us was the Sheslay River valley we had just climbed from. Looking southeast, we could see the valley we had been travelling along the past few days.

The landscape had changed at this high elevation. Now there were more willows than trees. That meant there were no blowdowns to be chopped through with axes, although the bushes offered their own challenges. With great effort, the horses pushed their way through thick willow, birch, and other shrubs. Most were chest-high to Sally even as she rode Outlaw.

"I thought it would be easier going here," Sally said when we paused for a breather. Being the shortest person on the shortest horse, Sally had the worst of the willows. They tried to drag, snag, and scrape her out of the saddle.

The horses seemed to like the willows, though. The branches and leaves brushed off the mosquitoes as the horses passed. I was glad that we had been talked into buying thick leather chaps at the tack shop months earlier; they prevented our legs from becoming scraped and bruised by the branches.

In some stretches the willows grew especially high, high enough to swat our faces as we rode past. The only way to continue north was to grit our teeth, duck our heads, and push our way through. The horses did the same, carrying us faithfully towards the Klondike.

SIX

Bogs and Blowdowns

On a map, swamps look rather inviting, with a dense cluster of little blue flowers on a patch of white. The map I was studying showed an endless string of blue flowers leading along the white valley bottom. The rest of the valley was coloured pale green, an area the key to the map referred to as "wooded area; unclassified scrub." I already knew what that meant.

"Where are we?" Sally asked.

"Right in the middle of a marsh," I replied, holding Blackie's reins in one hand and the map in the other.

"I know that, but where's the trail?"

After orienting the map with the compass, I checked our position against the mountains. According to the map, the trail wound right through the white area with the little blue flowers.

"Well, at least we know where the trail used to be," Sally commented dryly. With the constant delays of clearing our way through the forests and searching for the trail in the flooded valleys, we were not making good progress. We began to realize that we would have to push ourselves and the horses even harder to make up for lost time. Already, I was beginning to worry we might not have enough food or time to complete the Stikine Trail.

"Let's go, let's go," I said impatiently after I had tucked the map into a saddlebag. I goaded Blackie with my heels, urging him into yet another stretch of bog.

This was our third day of negotiating swamps, muskeg-laced valleys, and beaver ponds. I had discovered that, among other things, Blackie did not like swamps. Every time we came to a wet area he stubbornly resisted stepping into the mud. Once in the mud he rushed through, often taking the deepest route in his haste. His attempts at lunging through each deep section to get them over with were not very successful or satisfactory for either of us.

One lunge caught me off guard when I turned in the saddle to urge Mare along. I came down hard, smashing my chest into the horn.

"Hunnph," I grunted, just before the next lunge caught my right leg on the swell of the saddle.

"Arrgh," I groaned. Another bruise for my collection. One more leap and Blackie reached firmer ground.

"Jeez," I muttered, dazed by the wild ride. We were now on a small island of grass in the middle of the bog. Sally was ahead of us on Outlaw, who carefully picked her way from tussock to tussock. I was jealous.

I nudged Blackie with my boots. Gently. His ears went back, his neck arched, and he walked stiffly towards the mud. Blackie's left foot went in without incident. His right foot followed, then sank up to the knee as he transferred his weight to it. I heard a loud sucking sound as he withdrew his left foot.

Blackie snorted and leaped backwards to the firmer ground we had been on.

"Whoa, Blackie! WHOA, BLACKIE!" I pleaded as I felt his body stiffen underneath me. Blackie backed up even more, driving Mare out of his way. To avoid getting tangled in Mare's lead line, I quickly threw it to one side. Mare took this as her cue to head across without us.

By now Sally had reached the far side and had turned to

watch the performance. I tried again. Blackie sank deep into the mud and gave one magnificent buck in an attempt to free himself. I executed an involuntary, sideways somersault in mid-air and fell face down in the mud. The mud softened my landing, but what a mess! I lay there, winded and gasping, with a fool of a horse still lunging and bucking about the swamp.

I sloshed over to where Sally was holding Mare and her own horses. Mud oozed from my boots, my chaps, and my jacket. In my hand was my prized cowboy hat, which had been trampled into the mud by Blackie. It was a misshapen, sodden mess.

Sally looked me up and down, suppressing a giggle.

"Could have been worse," she said, "could've been me!"

That phrase was to become rather overused during the following weeks.

After we had traversed several more swamps, Sally came up with a scale to rate my performances. A one-star crossing meant that Blackie sank only up to his knees. A two-star rating was awarded when he lunged ahead, but I managed to remain in the saddle. A three-star event was when I was thrown from Blackie and landed face down in the swamp, inhaling muddy water delicately scented with moss, Labrador tea, and, if I was extremely unlucky, manure from the other horses.

Over the next days, I learned the hard way that the swamps were deceptive and not easily read. At least, not until I was in them. Sometimes there was solid footing under the moss. In other places the horses sank into deep, soft muck. After several more three-star crossings, I decided that Sally should lead through every swamp.

"You go ahead and tell me what it's like. Should I walk or ride?" I said to Sally one morning.

Outlaw was slow and sure-footed as she picked her way across the swamp.

"You can ride; it's not deep," Sally shouted from the other side.

Blackie seemed to sense that if the other horses could get

through, it might not be so bad after all. For my part, I tried to be more careful about my reactions. I was beginning to understand that when I became tense, Blackie became high-strung, expecting a problem. This time, I remained calm and cool and Blackie reacted the same way. Though pleased, I couldn't help wondering whether this meant that I had been partly to blame for all my muddy dumpings.

Sally cut into my thoughts. "Walk!" she shouted. We had reached a bog with soft spots that would spook Blackie.

I had to be quick. I swung out of the saddle before Blackie had time to think about the mud and start lunging. I gave him a hearty smack on his rump to send him across behind Outlaw and Dusty. Then I tied Mare's lead line out of her way and sent her across as well.

This time I had an uneventful bog crossing. Only my feet and pants became wet and muddy as I waded across to where Sally and the horses waited for me. I kind of missed the excitement of riding a bucking bronco.

"That worked well," I said. "At least I had a choice of which half of me I get wet!"

Sally was sympathetic, but couldn't really do much to help me other than try to choose the most suitable routes. For the entire day my pants were wringing wet, my boots filled with muddy water. That evening I warmed up by a roaring campfire and contemplated my fate; here I was surrounded by endless swamps with a horse that couldn't be ridden through mud.

Sally tried to be comforting. "Well, with every adventure comes a little misadventure."

"Easy for you to say," I interjected irritably. My legs were raw from the wet chaps, my feet both chilled and itchy. Sally was dry and mud-free.

"Hmmm," she murmured non-committally. I guess she knew me well enough to see that I needed to be left alone to sulk. She was kind enough not to remind me that the horseback part of our trip had been my idea. In a few minutes, I heard her preparing dinner.

I stared over my toes into the fire, wondering if I'd been

crazy to undertake such a long trip with so little riding experience—and with such a horse! It wouldn't have been so bad if we'd passed the worst of it, but I knew that ahead of us, day after day, was swamp.

As I sat gazing into the fire, a mug of tea and my favourite supper of macaroni and cheese helped to put me in a better frame of mind. A double ration of chocolate completed my attitude adjustment. After all, we had come for the adventure and we were getting it in full measure.

We spent the last part of the evening in the tent, looking at the map. I pencilled in our day's progress and marked our camp on the sheet.

"Only five miles," I announced. "Of course, we did spend two hours in the mud and another two hours trying to find the trail."

We were disappointed with our progress. Most days we were up at six and didn't go to bed until nearly midnight, and yet we had averaged only seven miles a day. We began to realize why so many gold-seekers had abandoned this route and headed for the Chilkoot Pass or White Pass trails.

I remembered reading one report printed by the *Winnipeg Daily Tribune* in 1897: "The route from Telegraph Creek to Teslin Lake was rougher than could be imagined. We were on the trail for thirty days, and during that time it rained steady for a week."

Conditions hadn't changed. It was still a rough trail, and it was still raining.

For three more days, we fought our way through an endless chain of bogs and swamps. Blackie wasn't the only horse to have troubles in the mud. We were winding our way through a bog one afternoon when Mare's lead line went tight, wrenching my right arm back.

"Whoa, Blackie." I turned to look at Mare. She hadn't followed our route, and now she was mired up to her chest in the muck. As she struggled to free herself, the sludge rose higher and higher until she had sunk to the base of the pack-boxes. Was there no bottom to the swamp?

I pulled on the halter rope. "Come on, Mare," I urged, as

she tried moving her front legs.

I looked ahead to Sally at the edge of the swamp.

"Care to tackle this one?" I offered in my most gentlemanly way, giving a sweeping bow from atop Blackie. Sally shook her head slowly.

"No, but thank you for the kind offer. Besides, you're already wet," she said. Once again, I dismounted and plunged into the muck.

After turning Blackie loose to join the other horses, I sloshed around to Mare's side. With all my strength, I heaved against a pack-box to break the suction of the mud. Then I tried rocking the packsaddle from side to side. I gave Mare several whacks on the rump and she began struggling in the mud, heaving, then thrashing her front feet, but to no avail. Finally, I waded in front of her and pulled on the halter rope again.

Nothing I tried would get her moving. Her eyes were glassy with fear, her nostrils flared as she struggled. Then she gave up. Her dark eyes looked straight into mine and I saw no fight left in them.

Just when I was running out of ideas, Sally came up with a plan.

"If you bring me a rope," she called, "maybe Outlaw can pull Mare out."

Once Sally was in the saddle, I handed her a long rope attached to Mare's halter. She wound it around her saddle horn.

"Okay, NOW!" I called. I whacked Mare's rump with a willow switch as Sally urged Outlaw forward. The line to Mare went taut. Then, with an impressive heave, Mare lunged forward. She thrashed about in the mud until she found better footing. Moments later Mare was with the others, eating grass.

"Look at that," I exclaimed when I joined Sally. "It's as though nothing happened." I felt exhausted as the adrenalin drained from my body.

Mare turned her head and nudged my shoulder gently as I checked her cinches. I rubbed her neck, taking time out to

Trail? What trail?

Which way?

pamper my packhorse.

"You had us worried for a minute," I said. Mare nickered softly. Although she could have no idea what I was saying, she seemed to understand my tone of voice.

The swamps and the bogs became, if not routine, manageable. Then we added a chain of beaver-flooded valleys to our repertoire. One in particular will remain fixed in my memory as a highlight of the trip.

Beavers had built numerous small dams that flooded the valley, and the trail became submerged under progressively deeper water. Sally went first, coaxing Outlaw and Dusty over a low dam and into water that came to the top of Outlaw's legs. I followed close behind.

As the water became deeper, Sally lifted her feet out of the stirrups to avoid getting water in her boots. I didn't have to worry about that because my boots were now permanently wet.

Suddenly, Outlaw pitched forward as her front legs sank into an invisible hole. Sally, perched high in the saddle with her feet out of the stirrups, catapulted over Outlaw's head and landed with an impressive splash in the pond. She came up spluttering and splashing.

Having been the ejectee for the past week, I'd never seen the humour in being dumped from a horse. Now I laughed until my sides ached.

Sally wrung out her hat, punched it back into shape, then squished it onto her head. The flattened, mud-soaked, wringing wet hat was the funniest thing I'd seen in days.

"Your hat looks a tad damp," I snorted.

I had just recovered the sense of humour that I had left at the bottom of the last mud hole. Sally slopped around miserably for a while, then the familiar twinkle returned to her eyes. Finally, muddy water still trickling down her face, she joined me in laughing about her unplanned swim.

"I'm wet now—might as well lead the way," she said, giving Outlaw a fond rub behind the ears. Sally plowed through the chest-deep water with her horses in tow.

That night we camped at the Nahlin River. We stood at

the river's edge, watching the water rush past. The river was wide and fast. This was one of the big rivers we had to cross and the ease, or lack of ease, with which we negotiated it would give us an idea of how we would manage on the bigger Nakina River. In Telegraph Creek people had warned us about the rivers. They had advised us to cross them later in the summer, when the dangers of high water had passed. But we couldn't wait that long—not if we were going to make it all the way to the Klondike before freeze-up.

In the morning we noticed that the Nahlin River had risen six inches during the night. The weather had been especially wet for two weeks and the resulting run-off had combined with snowmelt from the mountains to swell the river. Like the stampeders, Sally and I had to keep moving. It was already the first week of July, and we were less than halfway along the Stikine Trail. After the horseback part of our trip, we still had to build a scow and float hundreds of miles to our destination.

Roaring water poured over exposed boulders, and the river was laced with whitewater from shore to shore. I watched Sally guide Outlaw so they were angling upriver against the current. This way they wouldn't be thrown off balance or washed down the river by the force the water. Although waves surged high on Outlaw's chest, Sally had learned her lesson and kept her feet in the stirrups. Dusty followed on a long lead line to allow him some freedom of movement in the water.

We were next. Blackie's small hoofs churned the water as he swam across the deepest part of the river. The sight and sound of the water surging against Blackie's chest unnerved me. Blackie's nostrils flared in and out as he fought against the current. As soon as his feet touched the bottom again, he rushed towards shore.

"Easy. Easy," I soothed with a low voice while I pulled lightly on the reins. Mare was still in the deeper water and she needed time to catch up.

Once out of the river, we stopped to tighten the cinches and check the loads. Luckily, the pack-boxes were waterproof. Although the horses were breathing heavily, they were calm and unfazed by the crossing.

I wasn't as steady as my trusty steed. "I'd like to keep riding. I need to wear off some of this adrenalin," I announced, urging Blackie up the trail at a fast walk.

We were unable to change out of soggy chaps and boots, so Sally and I added sweaters and scarves to keep warm. Our wet chaps stuck uncomfortably to our wet saddles as we rode. Gradually our pants and chaps dried from the warmth of our bodies.

The trail led us steadily uphill through a tangle of mature willows that towered over our heads. As always, we concentrated on following the faint trail. Blackie shone at this task. He could follow the pencil-thin line of a trail, even when I couldn't see it through the brush. He was also much faster than Outlaw and stepped out at a brisk pace.

For one brief day, we were able to follow a fair trail through the forest, then the trail once again became a chain of bogs and bottomless swamps. Now and then, chopped willows indicated that someone had passed this way long ago. New growth from the decapitated bushes all but obliterated the route.

"We'll have to clear this," Sally said from somewhere behind me. "I think it's too thick for Dusty and Mare to push through with their boxes."

We slogged along for hours, making little progress as we led our horses through a maze of willows. Our faces became streaked with mud and sap, our arm muscles objected to raising an axe even one more time. At one point, Sally tripped on a root and fell headlong into a thick clump of willows.

I looked over to Sally. Through the day, I had watched her shoulders sag until she was hunched over the saddle. Now she looked close to tears. Wordlessly, we tied our horses to trees.

"Hey, Sal," I said, wrapping my arms around her. This was not like Sally to get discouraged, although I had to admit things were looking pretty grim.

We battled our way north, bush by bush, swamp by swamp. Each day, we advanced only two miles towards our objective. This is what it must have been like for the Klondikers who had been lured north along this route, believing it was the fastest and easiest way to the gold-fields. From clerks and bank tellers to train conductors and carpenters, they'd blundered onwards, cursing those who had said a good trail existed.

At one swamp, Sally and I lost the trail completely. We left the horses tethered to trees and hunted for stray axe-cuts that might indicate a trail. The last vestiges of this route to the Klondike had vanished. It had been swallowed up by a century of willow, aspen, bog, swamp, and beaver ponds.

Sally and I prepared to scout in different directions to search for a trail, any trail.

"Let's meet back here in half an hour," Sally said as she set off.

I returned utterly dejected, and collapsed beside Sally. "I couldn't find any sign of the trail. The trail report we've been using says we've done the easiest part of the route. It only gets worse. Now what?"

"I'm not sure," she mumbled.

I remembered reading about a man who hanged himself somewhere on this route because everything had gone wrong. Another stampeder, Stratford Tollemache, had written: "I have nothing good to say about the Stickeen Trail. It had been considerably advertised as being the best, although it turned out to be about the worst."

It was several minutes before I had the energy to ask Sally if she had seen anywhere to stake the horses for the night.

"No," she replied, her voice barely above a whisper. Her eyes were half-closed. It looked as though she wouldn't mind spending the night leaning against this tree in the rain.

"Then I vote we return to our last camp and decide what to do next," I said.

We retraced our steps in silence. As we rode back I turned things over in my mind. So far we'd had done the "good" part of the trail. How many days of non-existent trail lay between us and our objective? Would the Nakina River be too high to cross? Would we have enough food to complete the trip? I tried not to think of the obvious conclusion. I still wanted to get to the Klondike by the Stikine route.

Blackie seemed to sense my subdued mood and walked without his usual fuss around all the obstacles. He even nuzzled me as I undid his breast collar when we arrived at our previous night's camp. I reached up and rubbed him behind the ears.

Once the horses were turned out to feed, we lit a campfire and stared into the flames. It was a long time before either of us spoke.

"If we can cut a new trail and if the Nakina is not too deep to cross, we might just make it—if our food holds out," I said.

"That's a lot of *if*'s," Sally replied, voicing what we both knew. We had started with five weeks of food and after three weeks on the trail we had travelled less than halfway. There was no longer any trace of the old trail.

After a few minutes of silence, she continued. "You know, most of the stampeders turned back and took the Chilkoot instead."

"Yeah."

"I've always wanted to tackle the Chilkoot," Sally added, leaning towards me for my response. I could tell she'd been thinking about this for a while.

"Well, we could go down the Stikine River and up to Skagway by boat," I said, slowly warming to the idea. "Now we know why most stampeders went that way—this route is hopeless."

Despite a long list of reasons for turning back, we were deeply disappointed. We dragged ourselves to bed that night, weighed down with the feeling of failure.

Perhaps our journey would duplicate the Klondikers' experience more than we had first realized. I grasped hopefully at this thought. After all, we were not abandoning our goal of reaching the gold-fields. We were just going to get there by a more roundabout route, as many others had.

SEVEN

Working as a Team

"Ready to go?" I asked Sally as I snugged up Blackie's cinch.

"Any time," came her half-hearted reply from where she was untying Outlaw from a tree. Although Sally forced a smile, I knew that she was feeling as depressed as I that we had turned around.

After looping Blackie's halter rope over the horn, I swung into the saddle and gave a gentle squeeze with my heels to urge him onward. Mare followed close behind us. We had done this countless times over the past weeks, and the four horses moved smoothly down the trail.

Gently, I pulled the rein across Blackie's neck to turn him onto the faint trail heading south. As the day passed, we made good progress through the forested stretches where we had cleared the trail on the way in. However, we still had to work at finding a route through the open country. We frequently lost the trail in the swamps.

As we neared one wide swamp, I reined in Blackie and waited for Sally to catch up.

"Do you remember which way to go?" I asked. I couldn't remember if we'd skirted around this swamp or if we had gone straight across.

"No. Let's see if Outlaw knows." Sally released the reins and let Outlaw have her head so she could take the route she preferred.

Outlaw turned to the left without hesitation. She took us around the swamp, directly to the trail on the other side.

"Pretty impressive," I said to Sally. Outlaw was turning out to be a terrific route-finder. All we had to do was keep her from being distracted by lush grass or tasty-looking flowers.

Sally and I dismounted when we re-entered the forest. I hooked Mare's lead line onto the horn of Blackie's saddle and set off leading Blackie. Walking gave our saddle horses a chance to rest, and Sally and I enjoyed stretching our legs. Besides, I didn't want to become permanently bowlegged. It was enough that my clothes and hat now looked the part of a trail-worn cowboy.

The Nahlin River was still in full flood when we reached it late that afternoon. We knew a good meadow was on the other side and pushed on through the rushing water. It was a treat to know what lay ahead and where our next camp would be.

After more than three weeks on the trail, Sally and I had developed an efficient unpacking routine. Moving quickly, we worked as a team with few words spoken.

"Ready!" I called over Mare's withers to Sally. That was Sally's cue to unhook the cinch and loosen the rope on her side. I had already untied the knot that held the double diamond in place.

Seconds later I heard, "Okay," indicating I could pull the rope off and remove the canvas tarp. After removing the top load, we unhooked the two pack-boxes. I could almost see Mare sag and sigh with relief when the saddle was removed.

While Sally brushed Mare's back and legs, I checked for blisters or sores.

"She looks fine," I reported. I was pleased that the extra care we took loading the horses each morning had paid off;

after weeks on the trail not one of the cinches or saddles had given the horses sores.

After Dusty, we unsaddled Outlaw and Blackie. All the horses were accustomed to this routine. They knew they had to wait until everything was unloaded before they would be turned out on hobbles to feed. In less than half an hour the horses were in the meadow, heads down and munching grass.

"Best time ever," I said, smiling to Sally. We stood hand in hand for several minutes, watching our trail companions graze.

"Remember when it used to take more than an hour to unpack them?" Sally asked. Our morning pack-up routine had also improved. We had pared our time from four hours to a respectable two hours to have breakfast, break camp, and load all the horses.

Our outlook was improving as well, but it was a few days before we overcame the disappointment of having to take another route to the Klondike. For us, the lure of adventure and gold was still as strong as ever.

As our plans for the next part of our trip grew, we began to enjoy the simple pleasures of long hours in the saddle. The days blended into each other with the rhythm of trail life. Ten days, eighteen bogs, and endless stretches of tangled willow later, we came to the infamous beaver pond where Blackie had fallen off the hill and into the water.

"I'm not sure I want to tackle that beaver pond again; it's downright dangerous," I said to Sally. We had been lucky crossing the pond the first time; sharp, beaver-chewed sticks poking up from the bottom were a hazard and could impale a horse as it waded past.

"How about scouting to see if there's a route above the bluff?" Sally asked.

"Okay, flip you for it," I replied, pulling a hoof pick from my saddlebag. "If the handle lands pointing south, you go. North, I'll head up the hill."

It took Sally an hour to scout the route.

"I made it to the place where we had turned around on

our way in. It doesn't look that bad after all," she reported when she returned.

We followed a faint game trail which angled up the steep slope. I leaned forward in the saddle, adjusting my weight to make it easier for Blackie. When the horses started to breathe heavily, we took a break. They rested with nostrils flaring, and sounded like noisy bellows as their sides heaved in and out.

Just below the bluff, we came to the point of no return. The footing was treacherous, and there was no way we would be able to turn the horses around. As we continued on the traverse, it became so steep that my uphill stirrup touched the ground.

I remembered what Slim had told us about crossing such slopes: "Let your reins go loose and allow your horses to look down to get their bearings." Fine, Blackie could look down if he wanted. I didn't dare. The one time I had, I looked straight down Blackie's side and saw only air. I sincerely hoped we wouldn't have a "rope-under-the-tail incident." This was no place for a rodeo.

Once we crested the hill, Sally and I dismounted for the trip down to make it easier for the horses. Now and then, I flicked the lead line to keep Blackie from stepping on my heels as we worked our way to the valley. Each time I heard horseshoes skidding on the loose gravel, I glanced back nervously, hoping Blackie wouldn't run me over.

"Easy, Blackie. Easy," I said in a soothing voice. The horses walked calmly behind us, taking slow, sure steps.

Just as we were almost at the bottom, Mare caught a horseshoe on something and pulled it partway off. The clicking sound alerted Sally to the problem.

Luckily, the horseshoes and equipment were in Mare's pack-boxes. In a matter of minutes we had her tarp and boxes off. Our time spent handling the horses and picking up their feet each night now paid off. I held Mare's head, whispering sweet nothings in her ear to keep her calm.

Sally braced herself under Mare.

"Foot!" she commanded, running a hand down Mare's

front leg. Mare obediently lifted her foot. Using a large plier-like tool, Sally clinched two of the nails tight to the hoof wall. Then she removed the loose nails and began pounding in new ones. As I watched her work I was glad we had spent the time learning these skills before the trip.

"Don't lean on me!" she groaned when Mare shifted her weight. I pulled Mare's head to the opposite side to shift her weight back on her other leg.

Once all the nails were set and clinched tight, Sally filed off the rough edges.

"Okay, let's hit the trail."

"Good job, partner!" I said admiringly, giving Sally a warm hug. We repacked Mare's load and were on our way a few minutes later.

Although the day's drizzle had turned to a downpour, we agreed to make a detour to a small lake we had seen on the map. We were eager to try our luck at fishing. Our diet of pre-packaged trail food was becoming monotonous.

"I can taste pan-fried trout already," I said to Sally when we stopped to clear a fallen tree out of our way.

"That's odd. All I can taste is mud and water," Sally replied as rain streamed off her sodden hat.

We became soaked as each willow leaf, laden with a spoonful of water, slapped our faces. The water trickled down our necks until our collars were cold and wet. Even so, the side trip was well worth the effort. As we came over a rise, we gazed upon the most picturesque lake we had seen on this trip.

The downpour stopped almost as suddenly as it had started and the air was rich with the smell of wet earth and moss. We found an ideal campsite by the water's edge and soon had the horses unpacked and turned out to graze. Sally and I stood side by side on the shore.

"The reflection is so perfect it's hard to tell which way is up," Sally said, studying the lake.

"I suppose it would be a shame to ruin the reflection by casting the fishing lure," I responded. Sally argued that it would be a shame to eat slop for supper again.

A camp on the Stikine Trail

Watering the horses

Even so, I hesitated, absorbed by the scene and sounds around us. The tinkle of horse bells was accompanied by the call of loons echoing across the water. A gurgling creek nearby added to the wilderness symphony. After a few minutes, I cast the line. Two casts later, I had hooked a trout and reeled in our supper.

There was plenty of grass for the horses, so we took the rest of the day off from travelling. We scrubbed our clothes and draped them across bushes to dry, then baked fresh bannock to go with the fish.

The horses stayed nearby, with heads down as they munched the lush grass. However, just to be safe we took turns being responsible for their whereabouts. They had tricked us several times—we knew that sooner or later they'd start to wander.

The sun came out and was so warm that we swam in the lake, then stretched out near the horses for a rest. They must have sensed our calm mood, for they hardly wandered as they grazed. Every now and then, I lifted my hat from my eyes to check on the horses, but they were as content as we were to take a break.

As Sally lay daydreaming, Outlaw wandered over and nuzzled her hat gently.

"Hi, Piggy," she murmured. Sally reached up to stroke her pony's nose. Watching them, I felt a sense of well-being. Although not all had gone well on the trip, this was what I would remember most—the tranquillity of the scene, with us and our horses coexisting peacefully.

A while later, Blackie joined Outlaw, and the two horses spent several minutes in mutual grooming. I was surprised because Blackie usually tolerated no nuzzling. He was like a grumpy old man and the others generally left him alone. Yet now, standing neck to neck, Blackie and Outlaw appeared to be best of friends. Using upper teeth they scratched each other on the neck, concentrating on the mane where the black fly bites were the worst.

After a rejuvenating overnight rest at the lake, we continued on our way to a clearing that we had seen more than four weeks earlier.

"I remember passing this by when there wasn't enough feed for the horses," Sally said when we reached the meadow. Now it was lush with plants and flowers at their peak. In mid-June there had been frost every night and the plants had only just started to turn green.

The horses ate like hungry men at a smorgasbord. Each one snatched mouthfuls of horsetails, daisies, all types of grass, and almost anything green or yellow or pink, from dandelions to wild roses. I watched Dusty deftly spit out a pink fireweed plant he'd bitten off with a mouthful of grass. Earlier in the trip, when there had been nothing better to eat, the horses had eaten fireweed and even willow leaves. Now they passed them by, searching for more succulent fare.

Heavy rain pounding on the canvas the next morning kept us in the tent. The horses didn't mind the rain and we left them where they were, while we spent much of our time reading and writing in the comfort of our canvas shelter.

When the storm passed a day later we set out into a refreshing world. I sat tall in the saddle, somehow not as tired as I had been when we were heading north. On the trail again, the horses stepped out in a lively manner. We were all energized from a day of rest.

As we rode I gazed in wonder at our spectacular surroundings. On our way in, we'd been so busy route finding and dealing with horse problems we never had time to fully appreciate the scenery. Now we had time. To my left a silvery stream wound through a carpet of green moss. And far to the right, through the trees, I could see the outline of the rugged mountains, some with snow still on their slopes.

Aside from a few mud-hole rodeos and rope-under-the-tail incidents to keep life interesting, our return trip went well. Then, while crossing the Little Tahltan River, Blackie suddenly lurched up, Lone Ranger–style, and started thrashing about. What could possibly spook him in the middle of a river? I had become used to his antics by now, and remained firmly in the saddle.

I glanced over to Sally and saw that she was having a bit of a rodeo ride herself. When Blackie finally splashed out of the river he stood on the shore breathing heavily. I looked back at Sally, wondering about the reason for the excitement.

"They're spooked by the fish," Sally called to me. Salmon were migrating up the river, swimming between the horses' legs.

The horses had taught us many lessons over the past weeks, and one was to always expect the unexpected. There was never a dull moment!

On July 26, we reached the first place we had camped weeks earlier after leaving Telegraph Creek. By the campfire that night, Sally leaned against me and began reminiscing about our journey so far. Although we had been disappointed at having to turn around and take a different route to the Klondike, we felt a sense of accomplishment after five weeks on the trail. As greenhorns, we had managed to return to the trailhead without any major mishaps. The horses, our outfit, and Sally and I had survived the rigours of the trail.

More than just travelling a long way, we'd had a taste of what the Klondike stampeders had endured on this part of their journey. Now we understood some of the challenges and hardships they had faced. In fact, not much had changed over the years: a horse was still an unpredictable creature, and a good diamond hitch and tight cinches were still the keys to having a load stay on all day. And the trail was still abominable.

Like most stampeders who left the Stikine Trail for the coast and took another route to the Klondike, Sally and I searched for someone to take our horses. Unlike those stampeders, we were not able to find even one person eager to buy our horses and start on the muddy route when we returned to Telegraph Creek. Fortunately, Reg Collingwood offered to find good homes for our trusty steeds. He even arranged for someone to pick up our horses and take them south.

With mixed feelings, we said goodbye to our four trail companions. They had been a source of pleasure and some frustration, and we had grown to appreciate each one for its particular strengths.

I brushed Blackie, lingering over his mane. Despite his failings in the swamps, Blackie had been a faithful saddle horse. He had carried me without complaint over the roughest terrain.

"You're a pretty good horse when all your feet are on the ground," I admitted. One ear cocked back to catch my words.

I looked over to Sally and saw that she was fussing over her horses as well. She had selected a handful of the choicest dandelions and was feeding them to Outlaw and Dusty. We would miss our four-legged friends.

Once our horses were on their way, Sally and I began to prepare for our journey to the Chilkoot Pass. Instead of horseshoes, halters, and packsaddles, our equipment would be hiking boots and backpacks. For us, the lure of the Klondike was stronger than ever. With new energy, we looked forward to climbing over the pass, building a scow, and floating to the gold-fields.

EIGHT

To the Chilkoot

"Klondike Ho—again," Sally said with renewed enthusiasm when we reached the coast after travelling downriver from Telegraph Creek.

We had just arrived in Wrangell, Alaska. During the gold rush, ships travelling north along the coast had stopped here to deposit stampeders bound for the Stikine Trail. The ships had picked up almost as many people who had abandoned that route and were heading to the Chilkoot instead.

Sally and I booked passage north on a ferry bound for Skagway, the destination for Klondikers heading for the Chilkoot Pass or White Pass trails. For two days as we travelled northward, we passed massive glaciers that flowed down the mountains to the sea. Along the shore, house-sized blocks of ice that had calved off the glaciers drifted with the current.

"The icebergs look like ships steaming up the passage," Sally observed as we stood on deck, gazing across the water.

"But the icebergs are probably more seaworthy than most of the boats during the gold rush," I replied. I remembered reading that, during the peak of the stampede, a motley collection of dilapidated freighters, coal barges, and retired whaling ships had carried Klondikers up the coast. Many of those boats had been hastily fitted with tiered bunks, then manned with inexperienced crews and rushed into service.

With the wind in our faces, Sally and I leaned over the railing and inhaled the fresh salt air. The view of the Inside Passage was entrancing. We floated by towering mountains, which dwarfed the ship as we passed in their cool shadows. At the end of long fiords, misty waterfalls cascaded from the base of sparkling glaciers.

As the ship steered into Lynn Canal leading to Skagway, the mountains closed in on us. Now the tree-covered slopes dropped straight into the water, where they reflected on the calm sea, turning it a deeper shade of green.

That night, Sally and I planned to sleep somewhere on the deck of the ship. There was a shortage of berths, but at least the Alaska ferry wasn't overcrowded like the ships that had carried stampeders. Some stampeders had resorted to sleeping on boxes, tables, duffle bags, and even on the bare deck.

"Shall we sleep in tent city?" Sally asked, referring to a collection of tents that fellow passengers had pitched on the rear deck.

"I'd rather not be under the smokestack," I countered. "Let's sleep on the floor inside."

Sally and I stepped over several bagged bodies in the forward lounge and stretched out our own bags in the last available space. It was crowded and stuffy, but reasonably comfortable. A hundred years ago, we would have had to tolerate the smells and sounds of a hold over-filled with horses, cattle, and dogs.

On August 3, the ferry docked in Skagway. We walked down a long gangplank, accompanied by many other backpack-toting travellers. In the early days of the gold rush there was no dock. Ships arriving at Skagway and its rival port Dyea, a little to the north, had merely anchored in deep water. From there, horses and cattle had been swung out over the sea and dropped into the water to swim ashore. Small scows had shuttled gear from the ship to wherever the tide reached at that hour.

"Can you imagine all your gear being dumped on the beach?" Sally asked, glancing at the mud flats at the far end of the docks.

"As if the people from the Stikine hadn't seen enough mud already!" I replied. I tried to picture the Klondikers picking their way through the mud, trying to find their outfits among the mounds of food and equipment belonging to hundreds of other travellers. Stampeders had to move their year's worth of supplies to a safe place before the tide swept in, flooding everything. What a way to start the trip!

Even though Sally and I hadn't planned on going through Skagway, we'd read plenty about it during our comfortable, dry days in the library. We knew that Skagway had boomed from little more than a collection of tents to a city as one ship after another arrived from the south with gold-fevered miners. And it was busy twenty-four hours a day with con men doing a different sort of gold mining. The unscrupulous Soapy Smith and his gang had ruled Skagway, and the town became infamous for its lawlessness.

Soapy Smith's gang had set up information offices with false information and fake maps. They ran gambling halls with rigged poker games and set up telegraph offices with authentic-looking equipment but no cable to carry the signal. If newcomers made it past these pitfalls, they still ran the risk of being robbed in the street. Unwary men lost their outfits and fortunes within minutes of arriving in Skagway.

Skagway seemed more settled now, so Sally and I set out to explore the town. Many buildings reflected the character of the gold rush and gave us a sense of what the town had been during its heyday. The clunk of our hiking boots echoed on wooden boardwalks as we made our way past old clapboard-clad buildings.

Like all gold rush towns, Skagway featured many bars and dance halls. As rain began drumming loudly on tin roofs, Sally and I ducked into the Red Onion Saloon. It was like stepping into the past as I opened the door to a room dominated by a long, ornately carved bar from gold rush days. The worn wooden floor creaked as we walked to a table. Gold pans and other mining paraphernalia adorned the walls.

"You know, for the purpose of research I think we should order a couple of beers," I said to Sally.

"Right," she agreed, warming to the idea. "Just to get the feeling of what it might have been like to sit in this saloon a century ago."

As we each sipped a cold one, I read the headlines of a newspaper framed on the wall. The *Seattle Post-Intelligencer* from July 17, 1897 announced: "GOLD! GOLD! GOLD! GOLD! Sixty-Eight Rich Men on the Steamer *Portland*. STACKS OF YELLOW METAL. Some Have $5,000, Many Have More, and a Few Bring Out $100,000 Each."

Another newspaper reported: "The Klondike is no doubt the best place to make money that there is in the world. All you need is a pan and plenty of water!" That was all Sally had to read to renew the symptoms of her gold fever.

Blaring headlines like that had led people to believe that they would find nuggets under every bush. Many people were so convinced of success that by the time they arrived in Skagway they had formed partnerships. They were certain they needed a partner. After all, it took one person to hold open the sack and another to shovel in the nuggets.

The next day Sally and I hiked to Dyea, the gateway to the Chilkoot Pass. Dyea also had become a small city during the gold rush, boasting streets and boardwalks and false-fronted buildings. Restaurants, saloons, gambling dens, and dance halls sprang up to serve the transient population. Now there was little more than a few planks and one wall of a building to suggest there had ever been a city where we stood.

We looked up to the snow-capped mountains towering above us. Which ones guarded the high and treacherous Chilkoot Pass? We had only one load to transport over the top, but those mountains looked high and wild. It must have been a daunting sight to stampeders. Each person had to move their ton of gear over the pass to Bennett Lake on their way to the Klondike.

I found it hard to imagine that thousands of gold-seekers had once passed through here. All was quiet now, except for the sound of gulls overhead. The hustle and bustle of the Klondikers packing their gear over the mud flats and the sounds of horses' hoofs on the rocky trail were gone.

I turned when I heard the sound of feet clattering along the rocky shore. A group of hikers, backpacks bulging, tromped towards the trailhead. If nothing else, the trail was still here, leading up the Taiya River valley towards the Chilkoot Pass. And for Sally and me, the dry, hard-packed trail was a sight to behold.

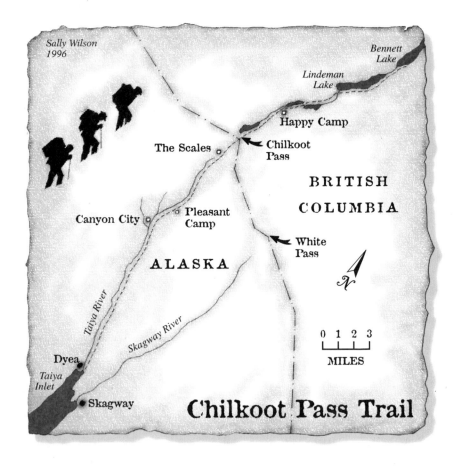

Sally Wilson
1996

Bennett
Lake

Lindeman
Lake

Happy Camp

The Scales

Chilkoot
Pass

BRITISH

COLUMBIA

Canyon City

Pleasant
Camp

White
Pass

ALASKA

N

Taiya River

Skagway River

0 1 2 3

MILES

Dyea

Taiya
Inlet

Skagway

Chilkoot Pass Trail

NINE

The Long Climb

I reached forward, lifted my heavy pack, and swung it onto my back. Then, like thousands of Klondikers before us, Sally and I began the long climb to the Chilkoot Pass.

"Only thirty-four miles to Bennett Lake," Sally said, rushing past me.

"You wouldn't start off so fast if you had thirty more loads to carry," I shouted after her. Stampeders who could not afford to hire packers had at least that many return trips ahead of them to get their year's worth of supplies over the pass.

Stampeders would stagger forward with a load for an hour or two, cache it beside the trail and return for another. Once everything was piled at the new spot, the weary men and women began the next relay. The ordeal of packing their outfits over the Chilkoot was so difficult that it took almost three months. By the time they had reached Bennett Lake, the distance travelled back and forth often added up to more than two thousand miles.

As I tightened my padded pack belt I thought of the ill-fitting pack-boards of that time, with thin straps that rubbed shoulders raw. Many of the gold-seekers probably had no idea what they were in for. If they were lucky, a fifty-pound load might have been a compact sack of flour or a crate of tinned meat or fruit. On other trips they would have had to labour under awkward loads of picks, shovels, whipsaws, sleds, or stoves.

At its beginning, the trail was easy enough as it led gently up the valley of the Taiya River. Sally and I walked through a coastal rain forest where giant cedar trees were draped with long strings of moss. Now and then, sunlight filtered through the branches. In places where the sun couldn't penetrate the thick canopy, the trail was dark and eerie.

The trail quickly became rougher and steeper. We squeezed between house-sized boulders, slipped over moss-covered logs and tripped on the roots of fallen trees.

"Sure would be nice to have our packhorses about now," Sally mumbled as we struggled up another muddy stretch of the trail. We missed our trail companions; I even missed Blackie and the way he made every mud hole an exciting experience. We now realized what a treat it had been to have them carry all our gear. Sally and I had crammed too many extras into our backpacks.

When we stopped for a rest, other hikers staggered past with their overloaded backpacks. Like travellers from years ago, we talked about the condition of the trail, the weather, and the weight of our loads. We learned from one couple heading in the opposite direction that it had been raining heavily farther up the pass. The trail there was slippery and treacherous.

During the stampede, trekkers would have shared a muddy, rutted trail with thousands of other gold-seekers. Now, a century later, Sally and I saw only a few other travellers. Even so, there was a strong sense of the Klondike spirit on the trail. Several people we talked with had been inspired by old journals. Some were following in the footsteps of grandparents.

On our first night, we pitched our tent with a cluster of others near the remnants of Canyon City. This clearing in the forest had seen thousands of campers at the peak of the rush. A steam boiler, a cast-iron stove, and some pots and pans were all that remained of this settlement. Anything fashioned from wood, whether log walls or wagon wheels, had rotted away and returned to the earth.

Looking at the stove, we conjured up images of a scene from a hundred years ago. Perhaps this stove been in a trail-side tent, the oven baking loaf after loaf of bread for hungry stampeders.

"I wonder how many pots of coffee had been brewed on the rusted stove-top?" Sally mused. "And how many wet socks and mitts had been hung to dry in its warmth?" If stoves could talk, this one would have an interesting story to tell.

The next day we came to Pleasant Camp, a level area in a sheltering grove of trees. It was indeed a pleasant place to take a break from the rigours of the trail. However, the next stretch of the trail was considered the worst section of the Chilkoot as it traversed dozens of creeks and led back and forth across the Taiya River.

"Ha! That bog was only ankle-deep," Sally said as she turned to watch me cross a wet section. Muddy water splashed up with each step and muck coated my boots. Even so, this trail seemed like a garden path compared to the Stikine Trail.

Stampeders had found travelling easier during the winter, when they could haul sleds or toboggans up the snow-covered trails, pulling two or three times what they could carry on their backs. Old photographs showed Klondikers hauling sleds loaded with such awkward items as cast-iron stoves, barrels, and boilers during the winter. Although winter dealt the gold-seekers many hardships, at least there was no mud to contend with.

The trail became steeper as Sally and I trudged through the thinning forest. Late in the afternoon we came to the edge of the tree line and the last good place to camp before the final climb.

"It looks like a stampeder's camp," I commented when we saw a tent city of eighteen tents in the clearing.

"All that's missing is a canvas-roofed restaurant with a sign out front," Sally replied.

"Or a guy beside the trail with a folding table and a card game in progress," I added, remembering stories of Soapy Smith's gang.

The small clearing was crowded and we had difficulty finding a good spot for our tent. I had to detour around tents and step carefully over guy wires, packs, and food bags when I went to fetch water for cooking. The roar of the Taiya River muffled many sounds of the busy camp: the unpacking of camp gear, the pounding of tent pegs, and the movements of people coming and going.

From camp, we had our first glimpses of the route up the pass. Rising from the plateau was a towering mountain of rock and rubble, leading almost straight up for almost four miles. I remembered reading an account of one gold-seeker who found this sight so forbidding that he immediately turned back.

At five in the morning Sally and I were the first campers to rise and break camp. Once on the trail, we soon reached timberline as the terrain changed from trees to bushes to bare rock. By mid-morning, we had reached The Scales, a level area just before the final climb to the summit.

The name was another reminder of the gold rush and the difficulties those before us had experienced. At The Scales hired packers had reweighed the outfits, and the fee for packing was renegotiated, often increasing as steeply as the slope ahead. It was a form of blackmail—Klondikers either paid the elevated price or packed their own supplies over the most difficult part of the trail.

Whether packing their own belongings or hiring someone else, stampeders stopped here to re-evaluate items that had seemed essential at the start of the trail. Sally and I sat on a boulder surrounded by items jettisoned from Klondikers' outfits: men's rubber shoes, high-top boots, and rusted pots. Pieces of broken pottery, glass, and rubber filled the cracks between boulders. We even saw picks and shovels that had been discarded along the way. It was like being in an open-air museum as we looked through the artifacts.

Sally placed her boot beside a woman's delicate shoe. The shoe featured endless eyelets and hooks for lacing up to the calf.

"It's like a slipper compared to my sturdy boot," Sally said.

"Imagine hiking up the Chilkoot Pass in shoes like that," I replied, looking up to the final pitch. Even with proper boots, the rocky slope would be hard on ankles and feet.

The pitch was so steep that fifteen hundred steps to the summit had been carved in snow and ice during the winter of 1897. These steps had been named the Golden Stairs by a Klondiker with a good sense of irony. Although the laboriously hewn stairs melted the following spring, this pitch is still referred to by that name.

Up and up we climbed. In many places, we had to reach out with both hands for balance as we scrambled over car-sized boulders. I thought back to photographs I had seen of a solid line of stampeders struggling with their burdens up this mountain pass.

Partway up, I stopped to cool my face with snow. Patches of snow still lay in the shaded hollows, more blue than white, reflecting the hues of the sky. In the valley below, ant-like figures moved towards us.

"That was hard work," Sally said when I joined her at the summit, almost thirty-seven hundred feet above the beach at Dyea where we had started. Sally was stretched out, using her pack as a pillow.

"It was a grunt. But to appreciate the Chilkoot experience to its fullest, I think you should do it thirty-nine more times. I'll wait here," I teased, prodding Sally's prone form with my boot.

After a short rest, Sally and I scouted around for a cache of boats we'd heard about. During the stampede, an entrepreneur had brought wood-frame and canvas boats up the pass to sell to Klondikers at Bennett Lake.

In a hollow off the main trail, Sally and I found bundles of wooden slats wrapped in canvas. Some were in neat

Along the trail

Chilkoot Pass

Old artifacts beside the trail

piles, others were strewn across the alpine meadow.

"They look flimsy, don't they?" I said to Sally. "Imagine anyone loading more than a couple of packs into one. I doubt they would have made it farther than the end of Bennett Lake."

"I'd rather take my chances in a scow," Sally said, thinking of the boat we planned to build.

Even so, sales would have been brisk, with people jumping at the chance to buy a boat instead of having to build one. The entrepreneurs had one slight problem, though. By 1898 the North-West Mounted Police were inspecting the outfits coming up the pass. These boats had obviously failed inspection and had been abandoned here.

The North-West Mounted Police had been at the summit to collect duty on items purchased in the United States. They also ensured that everyone had enough food and supplies for a year. There had been reports of near starvation in Dawson City. Gold-seekers without enough supplies were turned back to Alaska before they entered Canadian territory.

I took one last look back down the Taiya River with its valley of green surrounded by snow-capped mountains. The view was breathtaking. Bands of glistening white snow and blue sky were divided by the dark, jagged crest of the coastal mountains.

On the north side of the pass, the landscape consisted of drab, grey boulders and grey mountainsides that had been scoured by glaciers. Still, it was a welcoming sight.

"From here it's all downhill. Only two days to Bennett Lake," I said, gazing northward.

"And from Bennett Lake, it's all downriver to the gold-fields!" Sally added.

When we took a break to rest our knees on the long descent, Sally read from Martha Black's diary of a century earlier. The words summed up the trials of this part of the Chilkoot Pass: "Down, ever downward. Weight of body on shaky legs, weight growing heavier, and legs shakier. Sharp rocks to scratch our clutching hands. Snake-like roots to trip our stumbling feet."

"I suppose she wore flimsy boots like those we found at The Scales," I guessed, lacing my own boots tighter.

Now and then on our descent, our trail became a coffee-coloured ribbon of mud leading across a white snowfield that lingered from the previous winter. When the trail levelled out, we walked across wet ground where snow-fields had drained into the valley.

"Argghh, a booter," Sally groaned when she sloshed across a puddle too wide to jump. Klondikers must have hated slogging through this section again and again, until their boots were soaked right through. Personally, it didn't matter much to me—I'd been well trained by Blackie.

Lower still, we pitched our tent in the shelter of dwarf spruce trees. This lush, green area was called Happy Camp. Here, the stampeders were happy to find a dry, sheltered place to set up their tents. After crossing the barren pass, they were also happy to find plenty of wood for cooking.

Sally and I sat on the bank of a creek with our tired feet soaking in the icy water. This creek, less than an arm's length wide, was the headwaters of the Yukon River. From here it grew to become the vibrant waterway that had carried so many people to the Klondike.

The Chilkoot Trail now followed the young river, and we arrived at Bennett Lake on August 10, four days after leaving Dyea. A century ago, this shoreline had been crammed with tent after tent. Here, stampeders from the Chilkoot were joined by those who had taken the White Pass Trail, and ten thousand people worked madly to build their boats. The forest had grown back now. Just the same, Sally and I stood for a moment listening. We almost expected to hear the grating of whipsaws, pounding of nails, and rumble of trees being dragged to the beach.

Most of the Klondikers who had rushed north during the fall of 1897 could not go any farther than Bennett Lake until spring. By late October the lakes and rivers had frozen. Thousands of gold-seekers had to spend a cold winter living in canvas tents until break-up.

By the time the Klondikers had built their boats, they thought the worst was behind them. They had survived the rigours of the pass and the torture of whipsawing green lumber for their boats. Now all they had to do was float a mere six hundred miles down a series of lakes, rapids, and fast water to reach Dawson City.

Sally and I looked down Bennett Lake, imagining the scene in May 1898 when the ice went off the lake. Within days, a flotilla of more than seven thousand hand-built boats had drifted past this shore. Because we planned to build our own boat and float down the Yukon River, we felt the same excitement the stampeders must have experienced at this stage of their journey. Within a day or two, we would cross from British Columbia to the Yukon, and on towards the gold-fields!

Ahead of us, though, was an obstacle that hadn't existed during the gold rush—a dam now stood where the Whitehorse Rapids had been. The infamous rapids would have been a breeze compared with today's two-storey plunge. It would be almost impossible to drag a cumbersome scow around the dam, so we planned to hitch a ride to Lake Laberge, farther downriver. From there, we would continue our pilgrimage to the Klondike.

TEN

Building a Boat

Like a scene from days long ago, our canvas tent was surrounded by piles of rough-cut lumber on the shore of Lake Laberge. Beside the tent was a collection of boat-building paraphernalia: a cross-cut saw, a wood plane, chisels, mallets, bundles of cotton, and a can of pitch.

Our old-fashioned tent and piles of gear and lumber looked a bit incongruous sharing a campground with colourful nylon tents and motor homes.

"The things we get ourselves into," Sally said, surveying the lumber.

"Would this be a good time to remind you that this was your idea?" I quipped as we stood there, a bit overwhelmed by the scope of our project.

Like many Klondikers, we had never built a boat before. Somehow, during the next couple of weeks, we would have to turn the pile of planks into a scow. For reference we had a selection of hundred-year-old photographs and Sally's notes from our boat-building lessons in Vancouver. The rest was up to us.

Sally and I had spent a few days in Whitehorse and bought rough-cut lumber from a local sawmill. It was already mid-August so we didn't have enough time to chop trees from the forest and whipsaw the logs into planks, even if we had relished the blisters. Stampeders who could afford the luxury had also bought lumber. Theirs came from entrepreneurs who had set up portable sawmills at the lakes.

Those who had to saw lumber by hand were faced with one of the greatest ordeals of their journey. Partners first had to search for suitable trees and drag them to the lakeshore. Then they rolled each log onto a raised platform and began cutting planks with a whipsaw. One person stood on top of the log and pulled the heavy whipsaw on the upstroke; the other stood below and pulled on the downstroke.

In 1898, Addison Mizner wrote: "The man on top has to be almost a tightrope walker with new back muscles to pull it through. The one below gets just as dizzy looking up and trying to follow the line, while he gets his eyes and mouth full of sawdust. I changed forty times with my brother the first day. Each time he argued that I had the best of it. . . . At the end of two hours we had half a board sawed, and he asked me if I was tired. Of course, I wouldn't acknowledge that I was nearly dead. He called me a 'big stupid dumb brute,' which started a slight unpleasantness."

I remembered stories of partners who became so enraged that they parted company without further discussion. Their outfits, from sacks of flour to stove and tent were divided down the middle and the men somehow continued to Dawson City. Perhaps it was best that Sally and I weren't whipsawing our own logs—we still had a long way to travel.

Sally and I had no diagrams to show how a scow was built, only my own rough sketches gleaned from looking at the old photographs. And we had the terse instructions of the North-West Mounted Police that were passed on to builders in 1897. They advised each novice boatbuilder: "Make your boats long and strong . . . the Yukon River is both. Don't start out in a floating coffin." Those seemed like wise words.

We did have one reasonably detailed description written by a stampeder, A.T. Walden. I read it aloud to Sally: "Freight scows had straight sides and were square at both ends, but sheered up like a barge . . . with a long heavy sweep at the end. They were decked fore and aft, with the middle open, and a plank around the sides to walk on. Each scow had a mast, rigged with a square sail."

"Okay, I've got the idea. Where do we start?" Sally asked, itching to get to work.

"We could put the different length boards into separate piles. Then we'll know what we have to work with."

Once we had sorted the lumber, I spread my sketches on the ground and anchored them with stones. We had already solved many design questions. How long would the scow be? That was determined by the length of lumber we had found—just over eighteen feet long. How high would the sides be? Two planks seemed about right. Like the boat described by A.T. Walden, our scow would have vertical sides. With a narrow deck fore and aft, the scow would be complete.

After one day of sawing, planing, and hammering, we had a framework for the scow. Then we selected the straightest planks for the bottom of the boat. To have a watertight boat, we needed the planks to fit as closely as possible.

It took many passes with the plane before most of the planks met most of the way. Then I planed a bevel on each board so there would be a V-shaped groove where they met. Finally, we fastened these bottom planks to the frame.

Sally prepared to hammer cotton into the eight seams on the outside of the boat. She picked up the wooden mallet that Clyde had given us at the end of our lessons.

"Clyde said this would bring us good luck," she said, turning the mallet over in her hands. It seemed like a lifetime ago that we had been at Britannia Shipyards learning how to caulk a boat.

On the ground beside Sally was a bundle of cotton that looked like an oversized skein of wool. Sally pulled on the free end and one long strand of cotton, as wide as my thumb, emerged from the bundle.

"Here goes!" Sally said with the mallet poised above the caulking iron. With a frown of concentration and a tentative tap of the mallet, she began to hammer cotton into a crack.

"Steady as she goes," I said encouragingly. "Just keep in mind that if the caulking is not perfect, your scow will leak like a sieve." For some reason, my pep talk didn't seem to relax Sally a great deal.

Using the iron, Sally scooped up another length of cotton. Then she hammered it in, leaving a small loop of cotton bulging out of the groove.

"I'm not sure how much cotton is just right," Sally said anxiously, as I looked over her shoulder. She had to judge how much cotton to use, depending on the width of the groove and the thickness of the cotton. Packed tightly, the cotton would prevent water from entering the boat, but too much cotton would leave no room for tar to be added later.

When Sally reached the end of the first seam, it looked as though she had planted a neat row of cotton balls on the bottom of the scow. She stood and stretched before tackling the job of hammering these tufts of cotton into the groove. She became more confident with each whack of the mallet and quickly drove in the last of the cotton. It looked perfect to me; there remained just enough room to pour in hot tar, which would seal the seam.

I turned to other projects and became used to hearing a solid *thunk* as Sally packed the cotton in. Occasionally the sound was hollow. We wondered about that, but since nothing seemed amiss we shrugged it off.

When Sally had finished a day later, I began the task of pouring hot tar over the cotton. The solid tar came in a large can, and I had already chiselled out pieces to be melted in small pots.

Wearing leather gloves that she had used on our horseback trip, Sally held a pot over the embers of the campfire. She added a few chips of tar at a time and let them melt slowly. The idea was to heat the tar just until it began to smoke. It gave off a noxious odour, not unlike hot asphalt or roofing tar.

"If you keep one pot to melt the tar I can pour with the other, trading pots when I'm ready," I suggested.

Just then, the pot closest to the fire burst into flames. Sally pulled the pot from the fire and added more chunks of tar to the flaming liquid. The flames continued to dance happily in the pot until she clapped the lid from our coffee pot over it.

"So much for the tar having a low flashpoint," Sally said, quoting the claim on the side of the can.

"You're supposed to stir it constantly!" I teased. This was a frequent comment of Sally's whenever I cooked. I usually burned whatever was in the camp pot by not stirring it.

"This is the worst smell in the world," Sally said, trying to stir while keeping as far away from the pot as possible. She was in shirtsleeves as she laboured over the hot coals of the fire; I wore a heavy sweater.

My job was equally difficult. Slowly, I tipped the pot to pour a bead of molten tar into the seam. If the tar was too hot, it bubbled wildly when it came in contact with the cotton and wood. Then it lay in a ribbon of bubbles, which I had to pop with a knife. If the tar was not hot enough, it became too thick and would not pour evenly.

Finally, we were ready to turn the scow over and start working on the sides.

"What's all that cotton doing there?" I asked when we checked the seams from the inside. Spilling out of many cracks was the cotton Sally had hammered from the other side.

"I didn't realize I'd pushed so much through," Sally sighed, plucking at the cotton. "I guess that's what all those hollow sounds were." With scissors we cut away the excess cotton and gently pushed the remaining bits back into the cracks. If we pushed too hard we'd force the tar out the other side.

"I think we'd better pour some tar on the inside too," I suggested. "Back to the tar pots!"

Caulking our scow

Fastening the planks

We had calculated our supply with Clyde's help and were fairly sure that we had plenty of tar and cotton for the task. Hopefully, we wouldn't have to resort to using strips of canvas and pine pitch as many Klondikers had.

Clouds had been gathering all afternoon and I rushed to finish this task before the rain fell. The rain held off until Sally was heating tar for the last seam. The first few drops of rain sputtered and spat as they hit the hot tar. Fine droplets of tar sprayed up, bursting into flames when they landed in the fire. With a canvas tarp over the boat for shelter, I hurried to finish the seam.

On August 22, our fifth day of work, we started on the sides of the boat. Our plan was to pre-build each side on the ground, seal the seam between the two planks, then attach each side to the scow. These planks were the full length of the scow and were very difficult to fit together. One side had a large gap in the middle, even though the planks met at each end.

"Well, it's not cabinet work," I said, trimming a plank with the axe. I spent the next hour planing the edge of the planks, slice by slice, until they finally met most of the way.

"This side will be a little short," Sally observed. We'd had to trim so much that one side of the scow ended up being an inch lower than the other.

While Sally caulked the side boards, I began heating up tar for the seams. As she neared the end of a seam, I walked around the boat to check on her progress.

"Do you think the cotton is packed tightly enough?" I asked, inspecting her work.

A loud sizzling sound interrupted Sally's answer. I had been so busy meddling in Sally's work that I wasn't paying attention to my own. I turned just in time to see the pot of tar I'd left on the fire smoking and sputtering as it boiled over. Clouds of black smoke billowed from the pot.

Being nearest to the fire, Sally ran to rescue the tar pot just as a group of hikers from the campground walked by. We must have been quite a sight. As the group approached, I was gesturing with a wicked-looking knife that I had been using to slice off pieces of tar. I was wearing my horse-trampled hat and a tar-stained plaid shirt. Wood shavings clung to my beard.

Sally, bits of cotton caulking adhering to her tar spots, was attending to the smoking tar pot like a seasoned old-timer. The gold pan lay at her feet, filled with nails, and our old-style hand tools were scattered about. We could have stepped out of an old sepia print!

Our visitors seemed quite impressed, and I couldn't help adopting what I hoped was the proper air for a Klondike boat-builder. A couple of them photographed us without a word, as if we were a museum exhibit from the gold rush. Finally, one summoned the courage to ask me where we were going.

"Dawson City," I replied.

Several of the group looked at the rough-hewn scow and shook their heads. I overheard concerned whispers about Five Finger Rapids.

In the Klondike days, travellers used to gather by the water's edge to give boat-builders a bit of advice. As soon as we were accepted as almost-authentic Klondikers, neighbours of the 1990s turned out to carry on this tradition. New friends dropped by with fresh bread and jam, cinnamon rolls, and garden-fresh vegetables. Being a day's walk from the nearest store, we greatly appreciated all the treats.

"Beats trail food," I said to Sally, biting into a warm cinnamon roll.

"Yup," she agreed. "Do you think we can drag out this boat-building project for a few extra days?"

By the end of day nine, we had completed the sides of the scow. Now, we had to turn the boat upside down so we could build the sloping bow and stern sections.

"How are we going to roll this hulk over?" I asked after we'd discovered that the two of us couldn't budge it.

"No problem, I'll find some volunteers," Sally replied. There was a shortage of visitors at that moment so Sally toured the campground. She returned with two

Starting to look like a boat

Ready for launching

strong-looking men who helped us roll the scow over.

Sally and I redesigned and modified our plans as the scow-building progressed. After looking at several old photographs, I came up with an inspired plan to reduce the number of seams we had to caulk at the bow and stern.

"All we have to do is lay three long boards crossways instead of nine short ones lengthwise," I said knowingly. It seemed odd that none of the scows in our selection of photographs had been built this way. Even so, we couldn't think of any reason not to take this shortcut.

Two more days of "cabinet work" and we'd completed the sloping ends. The scow, now considerably heavier, was flipped over for the last time with the help of four volunteers. With thoughts of the big waves and wild rapids ahead, we covered a section of the bow and stern so that waves could wash over the scow without capsizing us.

Then we added several strips of wood to form a platform to stand on. Someone had suggested that if we walked directly on the bottom of the boat we risked pushing the boards off. That would be a memorable event if we were in the middle of the river at the time.

We planned to use two oars for rowing and a long sculling oar at the rear of our scow for steering. Two wooden pins served as guides for the sculling oar. For good measure, we added a pair of pins at the front, just in case we became turned around in the current while trying to run the rapids.

Our next project was to test various seat heights until we found one that felt about right for rowing. Then we were faced with the problem of where to position the oarlocks. With the oarlocks temporarily pegged in position, I sat in the boat and pretended to row. I hoped to get a feel of where the oarlocks should be placed.

"Faster, faster," Sally urged. With the oarlocks creaking loudly, I was making great imaginary speed along the gravel. Then one of the campers who had wandered past a few days earlier came by again. One look at me and he turned mid-stride and headed the other way.

"And I was just going to ask him to swim over and help out," Sally said, collapsing with laughter.

Our last project was to rig up a square sail to take advantage of the winds that blow down Lake Laberge. In the early days of the gold rush, a colourful armada of boats was rigged with sails fashioned of anything from striped Hudson's Bay blankets, canvas tents, or mackinaw coats, to pairs of long underwear sewn together. We had no extra blankets and needed our long underwear for the cold days ahead, so our sail would not be as colourful. Instead, we would use a mud-stained canvas tarp that had covered the pack-boxes during our horseback trip.

"Where should the mast go?" I asked Sally. She was the resident expert. Her experiences of sailing a small dinghy several times as a teenager were more extensive than the sole outing I'd had.

"I don't know. What can you see in the old photos?"

"Can't tell, really."

"I think the scow would nose-dive if we put the sail in the bow," Sally said. "Let's put it in the middle of the boat."

I argued that the mast would be in the way there, especially if we had to change seats to face the other way. We finally agreed that it should not go between the centre seats, but just forward of them.

With the mast installed, the scow was complete—only two weeks after we had planed the first plank. Our craft was eighteen feet long and six feet wide. Although it looked more or less like a packing crate, it appeared strong enough to withstand the four-hundred-mile journey. Or so we told ourselves.

We had no sooner finished sanding the last rough spot on the seats, when our friends Doug and Fran from Whitehorse dropped by. They arrived just in time to help us move the scow. We rounded up a couple more volunteers.

Even with four other people helping, we had difficulty carrying the boat, partly because of its awkward shape. As we struggled forty paces to the lake, I guessed our scow weighed as much as a grand piano.

"How much water do you think this hulk will draw?" Doug asked, puffing when we finally set the boat down at the edge of the water.

"We should take bets," Sally suggested.

Estimates from our friends varied from two inches to twelve. The latter estimate, stated with authority, was not encouraging—the high side of the scow was only sixteen inches from top to bottom!

"You know what they said about a well-built river boat— they were so shallow in draft they could float on a heavy dew," I said. To the snickers of Doug and Fran, I suggested our craft would easily fit this description.

Doug had the last word. He walked over and eyed our finished scow critically. "What makes you so sure it will even float?" he whispered in my ear.

The Yukon River

Wind and Waves

A small but enthusiastic crowd of friends looked on as Sally and I christened our craft the *Yukon Belle*. We decided against actually cracking a bottle against the bow—it would be a poor start to put a hole in the scow before it was even in the water.

Once in the lake, *Yukon Belle* not only floated, it drew barely an inch of water. Sally and I stood proudly beside our new boat, and I ran one hand along the gunwale while our friends took photographs. I hoped no one noticed me wince as a sliver from the rough wood pierced my finger.

I followed Sally into the boat and pushed us from shore with the long sculling oar. As we drifted away, a cheer went up from our friends. I recalled the words of Tappan Adney during the gold rush: "When a boat is ready to be launched everyone turns in to help. And when a boat departs it is with shouts of good wishes and a fusillade of revolver-shots." These days a fusillade of shots was out of the question.

"It's still floating!" Doug called out, feigning disbelief.

I put my weight into the oars, testing their strength, and the scow responded by gliding smoothly across the water of Lake Laberge. To my delight the scow manoeuvred easily, turning with the mere dip of an oar.

As I continued to row, Sally noticed droplets of water on the floor. No problem, we decided; they must have come in on our rubber boots.

Ever so slowly, the droplets became small puddles.

"We're leaking!" Sally said in a whisper, not wanting to alert our admiring onlookers. After all those hours spent banging cotton into the seams then pouring pitch inside and out, how could the scow possibly leak?

We could hardly believe our eyes: water was seeping from each knot. We hadn't even considered that possibility. And there were many knots in the rough wood, each spouting a mini-geyser of water.

"The good news is, the seams aren't leaking," I called to our shore-bound onlookers.

"The bad news is, water is pouring in through the knots!" Sally added.

"The wood just needs to 'take up' a little," I confided knowingly to Doug when we returned to shore. We had been told that dry wood needs to soak up water and swell before a boat becomes watertight. I secretly hoped this was the case with ours. We left the boat in the water that night to "take up" and prepared for the start of our journey the next morning.

On September 2, our day of departure, the scow seemed to have quenched its thirst. At least, it was no longer drinking great gulps of lake water. There was only a thumbnail's depth of rising damp in the bottom. That was good enough for us— we bailed out the water, then loaded our waterproof duffle bags, boxes, and canvas tarps into the scow.

"It's lucky we built a big boat," Sally commented as the scow filled up with gear. We pushed the scow into knee-deep water to prevent it from grounding, but we discovered this was not necessary. Even fully loaded with one month's supplies, *Yukon Belle* drew just over two inches of water. That left more than thirteen inches of freeboard, enough to allow moderate waves to pass without swamping our scow.

As soon as we were away from shore, I heaved on a rope

and raised the canvas tarp against a blue sky.

"Klondike Ho!" I shouted to the wind.

"Hey, that's my line," Sally said. The sail filled out with the morning breeze, pushing us down the lake.

I turned for one last look at the beach where we had built our boat and noticed that we were already sailing fast enough to leave a wake behind the scow.

As we rounded the first point on the west side of the lake, we were beginning to feel rather pleased with our progress. The scow hadn't sunk, the oarlock screws hadn't pulled out of the planks, and we were making fine headway. And the wind was in our favour.

The wind picked up through the day, eventually creating rollers that propelled us down the lake at an exhilarating pace. The square sail strained against the lashings and the guy ropes from the mast were guitar-string tight. Sally and I whooped and hollered, thrilled by the speed as we surged forward, carried on the crest of each wave like a long, pine surfboard.

Grinning wildly, we congratulated each other on our boat-building skills. Our craft might have looked like a box to any onlooker, but to us it was a sleek racing sloop. I wouldn't say the boat was planing across the water; however, it was certainly plowing through it in a respectable manner.

Since I couldn't see around the wind-filled sail, Sally did the navigating. She was positioned where she could duck under the boom and look ahead.

"I think we should steer closer to shore," Sally called. "Those waves are getting big!"

She began to glance back, a bit anxiously I thought. When she became uncharacteristically quiet, I looked back at the rollers. Wind-driven whitecaps now threatened to break over the stern. I could feel the power of the waves as each lifted and twisted the scow. Even though they came close to spilling over the sides, I wasn't too worried. In fact, after weeks of plodding along muddy trails, I relished a bit of speed.

When waves started to splash over the rear deck, however, I began to take things more seriously. This was a

The inaugural float

Waiting for the wind

large, unforgiving stretch of water, especially for a not-entirely-watertight hand-built scow. It was also a poor place for a dunking. The green, crystal-clear water was hardly warmer than the ice that remains on it until early summer.

While building the scow, we'd watched the lake and noted its many moods. A strong wind from the north or south would often come up without warning and whip the lake to a frenzy of choppy waves. Several times, the waves had built to boat-swamping height within minutes.

We steered as close to shore as we dared, keeping just out from the rocks. Scanning the shoreline, Sally searched for landing spots, knowing that the wind could reach gale force at a moment's notice. Finally, she spotted a sheltered bay.

Sally pulled hard on the sculling oar and we cut across the waves for shore. I dropped the square sail just in time to see an offshore rock in our path.

"Left!" I called over the roar of wind and waves. Sally pulled the sweep to the left, which aimed the boat to the right. I had meant for Sally to steer to the left. Unfortunately, we hadn't worked out our communications in advance.

"The other left!" I shouted as the rock loomed closer. Sally pushed the sweep right and the boat swung the other way, just missing the obstacle.

Finally, we were washed into the small bay. As the danger passed, I exhaled slowly, thinking of the many Klondikers who had perished in the frigid waters. Possibly, in their eagerness to reach the gold-fields and with so many hardships behind them, they had forgotten to treat the lake with caution. Sally and I chose to err on the side of safety.

By noon of our second day, the wind dropped . . . completely. Until mid-afternoon we lounged in the scow and rowed a little to keep busy. Mostly, we just soaked up the sun, enjoying the rest. The silence was so complete that we felt the hugeness and isolation of the lake and land around us. The only sounds were the splash of the oars and the low creak of the oarlocks. We found ourselves unconsciously breaking the silence, whistling a tune or singing.

Without warning, a strong wind came up around mid-afternoon. Although we'd recently passed a good campsite, it was impossible to row back against the rollers. We continued northward. Minutes later we were moving fast enough for the scow to push up a wave in front and leave a wake of turbulent water behind.

Once again, we needed to find a sheltered cove to protect the scow. The map showed this west shore featured many coves. What the map didn't show was that these coves had no suitable beaches to land the scow, and no clearings large enough to pitch a tent. Neither of us fancied spending the night curled up on the hard seats of our boat.

"Let's land over there," Sally suggested, pointing out a tiny bay I hadn't seen. The pebbly beach looked inviting. Calmer water indicated that the high bluffs afforded good protection from the wind and waves.

As we pulled into the bay we saw that the beach was very steep, with pebbles pushed up by the relentless force of oncoming waves. We would be unable to pull even a corner of the scow out of the water.

"This'll have to do," Sally said. "I don't want to venture out on the lake again. It's too dangerous."

"You've talked me into it. Besides, there might not be a better place farther on."

Sally jumped out, taking a rope with her. The pebbles gave way under her feet and she scrambled up the loose surface using her hands for balance. The water wasn't quite as calm in the bay as it had appeared from a distance. *Yukon Belle* rose up with each wave only to be dropped, crashing down with a shudder onto the pebbles. Using sticks as makeshift tools, we scraped out a hollow for the scow to nestle into.

While Sally organized camp, I started my nightly routine of bailing out the scow with the gold pan. After fifty scoops, I stopped counting. There seemed to be lot of water, but there was no way to tell which seams were leaking or which knots were still seeping. The scow had been in the water for almost three days and I was beginning to wonder if it would ever "take up."

During the night I woke to a rhythmic crunching; it sounded as if someone was shovelling gravel into a wheelbarrow just outside the tent.

"Sally," I whispered, nudging her. "Do you hear that?"

"No," came her mumbled reply.

I remembered a similar exchange just before we discovered our horses had run away. Listening more intently, I realized that I was hearing the sound of waves crashing against the gravel beach. The hollow grinding noise sounded like the scow battering into the shore.

"I'm going to go check the scow," I announced, unable to endure the suspense any longer.

Down at the beach, I found *Yukon Belle* being pummelled by waves. During the night the wind had switched from the south to the northeast; the waves were now coming straight into the bay.

I started back to the tent to rouse Sally, but she was already out the door, a beam of light from her headlamp leading her towards me.

"It doesn't sound good," Sally said as she approached. She always was good at understating disasters.

Sally and I took turns standing in the water to hold the scow off the shore while we discussed our predicament. The scow was beached in a small, curving bay, not much larger than a swimming pool. Although we couldn't see the other side of the bay in the black night, I thought I remembered seeing a lone tree on the point.

"Let's try stretching a rope between the tree on the point and the shore on this side. Then we can tie the scow to the rope and keep it off the rocks," I suggested. It was our only option, other than spending the night in the icy water holding the scow off the shore.

I tied all our ropes together into two lengths. With the shorter length, I secured the right corner of the bow to a tree near us. While Sally held the boat, I set off along the beach, trailing a length of rope tied to the stern. I hoped the rope would be long enough.

I crawled over the slippery rocks to the point, groping my

way forward as spray from the crashing waves washed over me. The roar of the pounding surf became louder and louder until it was all-consuming. I neared the end of the rope, and the bucking scow threatened to pull it from my hands. Finally, the thin beam of my headlamp caught the gnarled trunk of a lone, tenacious pine on the point. There it was! I tied the rope around the base of the tree. There was barely a hand's length to spare.

It was four o'clock in the morning and still dark, but I knew we would worry too much about the scow to sleep. We lit a fire on the beach, and by its light we kept an eye on the pitching form of the boat. The wet wood in the campfire crackled and sent off showers of sparks, cheerful and heartening against the gloomy night. The flickering firelight illuminated only the boat, the beach, and the bluff bordering the lake. Nothing else. We sat by the fire, sipping our hot chocolate and waiting for dawn.

Gradually, the morning grew brighter. Just before six o'clock we broke camp, packing quickly. By the time I had tossed the sleeping bags out the door, Sally had carried the other gear down to the beach. Together we folded the canvas tent.

We tied our gear into the scow and rowed out to open water, away from the rocky shore. It took us nearly two hours, straining against the oars, to row back to a suitable bay—the one we'd passed at three o'clock the previous afternoon!

"Looks like we'll be spending the day in the tent," I said as I watched storm clouds build on the horizon.

"That doesn't sound all bad," Sally replied, nestling against me.

The wind grew in its fury and we had no choice but to stay where we were. For most of the day, we lay in the tent listening to the storm: the hissing of wind in the trees, the flapping of the canvas walls, and the muffled rumble of rollers breaking on the beach.

That evening I bailed out the scow as usual. Every now and then I scooped out water bugs, and hoped they had come in on our boots and not through holes in the boat. They were black, beetle-like creatures that used their narrow wings to propel themselves through the water. I decided to keep an eye on our small stowaways; if they ever abandoned ship I would worry about the seaworthiness of our vessel.

It was then that I noticed that the screws holding the sides to the frame of the boat were visible between the boards. As the floorboards soaked up water they had expanded, pushing the sides out a thumb's width. Luckily, the seams still looked watertight. Even so, with almost four hundred miles to go I was worried. I decided to wait awhile before mentioning this new development to Sally.

As we strolled along the beach after supper, we came across the wreck of a small boat with a boot-sized hole in the hull. It made us pause, thinking of the narrow escapes we'd had already. Although the boat was sturdily built with lapped planks over a strong frame, it had come to its end on the lake.

"I'd say that's a sign we shouldn't push our luck," Sally commented grimly.

I agreed wholeheartedly. Klondike journals were peppered with stories of boats that had been lost on the big lakes.

The next day brought calmer weather, with just enough wind to fill our sail and take us to the end of Lake Laberge. In the safety of unruffled water we rowed for two hours to reach the outlet.

While Sally took her turn rowing, I spread out a map and looked over the route ahead. The names on the map fascinated me, and I followed them downriver, northward. There was Fourmile Rock, Gold Digger's Point, and Scow Bay. My finger tracing the blue line of the river, I visualized the scow drifting past each landmark.

As Lake Laberge narrowed near the outlet, the current picked up, almost imperceptibly at first, then with the rushing momentum of a river. From here on, our scow trip would change character. We no longer had to depend on the whims of the wind. For the rest of our journey, we would be carried by the current of the Yukon River.

TWELVE

A River of History

As the scow swept down the Yukon River, Sally tested the oars, becoming accustomed to how *Yukon Belle* handled in the current.

"Rock ahead!" I warned, then steered hard with the rear sweep. Fortunately, the heavy scow manoeuvred well in the current. With the combination of oars and sweep, we were able to dodge in and out among the boulders.

"Not bad," I said. "A well-designed boat, if I do say so myself."

"Actually, I think it has more to do with my skill at the oars," Sally countered. Whatever the reason, we were pleased with the scow's performance.

It wasn't long before we discovered that the current tried to sweep us to the outside of each bend and into the bank, where rocks would grind our boat to sawdust. We struggled to stay mid-river and took turns reading the water: a hump indicated a boulder beneath the surface; choppy waves meant shallow water; and a rhythmic splashing might be a submerged tree waiting to snag our craft.

This swift, narrow stretch of turbulent water was one of the most dangerous parts of the Yukon River. During the stampede more boats sank and more outfits were lost here than on any other stretch of the route. Many of the bends, creeks, and rocks were named after boats that had been wrecked or the people who had drowned there.

Casey's Rock had been named after a Klondiker who managed to get over the Chilkoot forty times, build a scow, and navigate the rough water of the upper Yukon River and Lake Laberge. Then, on this section of the river, he rounded a corner and struck a rock head-on. He lost all in the wreck. Undaunted, he returned on foot to Dyea. There, he secured more supplies and trekked over the Chilkoot forty more times with his new outfit. He built another boat and for the second time survived the canyons and rapids, as well as the treachery of Lake Laberge. Then, coming around the same corner of the river, he hit the same rock and lost all again. Casey was so upset he took his life on the spot.

As I was thinking about Casey's misfortunes, there was a shuddering crash and I found myself sprawling across a mound of duffle bags. The scow bounced out of the water as if pushed by an unseen force from below.

"Do you think that was Casey's Rock?" I groaned, looking up at Sally.

"No," Sally said, glancing at the map. "But I think I'll name it Ian's Rock to commemorate your abilities as a lookout."

If our boat had been much larger or heavier, the boulder might have driven a hole through the bottom. Fortunately, a quick inspection under the floor slats revealed no visible damage to the hull.

Keeping a closer watch for obstacles, we drifted with the current, letting the river do most of the work. It sped us along at nearly six miles an hour. We didn't actually travel forward that distance each hour because *Yukon Belle* never travelled in a straight line—the scow was carried here and there by the whim of the current, often sweeping towards the outside of each bend. Now and then, we had to row feverishly across the river to avoid obstacles.

I pulled out a copy of a map that had been used on the

river during the gold rush. Now that Sally and I were actually here on the river, not far away in some library, we could see the terrible difficulties that these inaccurate maps could lead travellers into. The map was not to scale and many obstacles were incorrectly marked. Stampeders had been forced to rely on rumours or reports from other travellers for information. Sometimes they learned about the rapids only when they hit them. That didn't seem to be an ideal way to run a river, so we put away the old map and referred to a more up-to-date river chart.

There were constant reminders of the river's history, from skeletons of wrecked boats to old cabins and clearings where woodyards had been. Sally and I often pulled ashore to explore places that caught our attention.

During our first landings, we began to develop the technique for stopping what was basically a huge, heavy box floating down the river. First, we watched for an eddy and steered towards it. The river was so fast that we could not have landed without the help of the slower water.

Our routine began with me rowing against the current to slow us down. Just before *Yukon Belle* crashed into shore, Sally would leap overboard with a rope in hand. I thought our system worked quite well—but then, I wasn't the one who had to leap out of a moving boat.

On one memorable occasion, Sally stood poised, holding a coil of rope in one hand. A split second before impact, she launched herself towards the shore, trailing the rope and yodelling for effect.

The line tightened. Sally leaned back, straining against the rope. As the boat bumped and scraped on submerged rocks, Sally was dragged along the beach, her heels grinding against the round pebbles, which offered little resistance.

I offered encouragement from my perch in the boat. "Pull harder!" I couldn't resist calling. Sally took the bait and, with one mighty heave, stopped the scow. Her boots had left deep gouges in the gravel.

"Why do I always have to be the one who jumps out?" Sally asked. I didn't answer, but flashed her an innocent smile. It seemed that she was on to me.

We spent that night by an abandoned cabin, which leaned precariously but charmingly over the water. Although the cabin was musty and dusty inside, it gave the impression that the last tenant had just stepped out for a walk. The coal-oil lamp, the Yukon stove, and the hand-hewn chair by the stove were all waiting for someone's return.

Inside the cabin, we felt the presence of the old Klondikers again. I thought of the photographs with the prospector whom Sally had nicknamed Iron Grip. Had he stopped here on his way north? What had his partner been like? I wondered what kind of boat he had built, and if it had leaked like ours.

Farther downriver, where the Yukon and Teslin Rivers merged, we thought of the stampeders again. Here the flotilla of boats was joined by the gold-seekers who had managed to traverse the Stikine Trail and float down the Teslin River. From here, they had only to float down the Yukon River to reach their long-sought goal. We felt the same anticipation they must have felt a century ago; the gold-fields were becoming closer with each oar-stroke, each set of rapids.

At this junction we passed the ghost community of Hootalinqua, where we found the remains of an old North-West Mounted Police cabin. Looking up Hootalinqua in the history book we kept handy, I learned that it was one of many police posts that had been along the river. They had served as a safety net for the stampeders who coursed down the river in their flimsy boats.

I read aloud a paragraph explaining that the Klondikers' boats had been marked with serial numbers. The serial number, along with the names of each crew member and their next of kin, had been registered with the police. If a boat failed to check in at the next post by a reasonable date, the police would send out search parties to comb the river.

I leaned over the side of the scow. "We should have painted a serial number on our boat," I said to Sally.

"A lot of good that would do," Sally replied with a wry

grin. "Your next of kin is right here with you."

From the junction of the two rivers, the scale of the Yukon River became more impressive and the volume of water increased. Stretches of turbulent water now became strong enough to grab the scow and turn it about, giving us a sense of the power of the river. Mountains in the distance gave a feeling of grandeur to the scene, very different from the closed-in feeling we had experienced along the forested shores upriver.

Sally and I took turns at the oars, occasionally steering the boat. Every hour or so, I bailed out for a few minutes. Our gold pan was the perfect tool for the task.

"If anyone saw you now, they would think you'd gone gold-mad," Sally said, flicking a few drops of water at me. "It looks like you're panning in the scow!"

Bailing was not as time-consuming as it had been, because we'd finally discovered the source of the leaks. My clever time-saving plan of installing the bow and stern planks crossways had backfired. The bottom planks had swelled as they absorbed water, pushing the sides of the boat out. Unfortunately, the bow and stern planks hadn't swelled in the same direction. As a result, there was a gap at each corner of the scow.

Luckily, we had followed the recommendations of an old guidebook. *Gold Fields of the Klondike* had warned: "Take plenty of tow for packing possible cracks in your boat, also two pounds of good putty, some canvas, and a small can of tar." So far, our morning's patch job with tar had stemmed the leak.

Not every day was spent just drifting and bailing. One afternoon we faced a strong north wind. The worst of the wind came in gale-force gusts, bringing slanting rain with it.

"I'm rowing as hard as I can," Sally puffed, each word punctuated by a heaving breath, "but we're not moving down the river. That large tree on the bank has been beside us for five minutes!"

"Let's trade places."

As I took my turn at the oars, Sally sat facing into the

Lunch on board the Yukon Belle

Scow Bay

wind-driven rain so she could see down the river. She leaned forward, hunched in her oilskin coat, her collar up and her hat pulled low. Rain poured off the brim and continued in streams down her jacket. Every few minutes she looked up to check that we weren't about to crash into something.

The design of our flat-nosed, broad-beamed craft made it difficult to make headway into a strong wind. At the first opportunity we pulled out of the current to wait out the storm.

Sally and I were chilled to the bone from sitting in the scow, despite our vigorous rowing. We took refuge under a tree near the edge of the river to watch the rain squall rush by. A campfire cheered us up and warmed numbed fingers and toes. Once the storm passed, we continued down the river.

When we neared a place named Scow Bay on our map, Sally insisted that we visit this landmark.

"With a name like Scow Bay, we have to check it out!" she said. "After all, ours is probably the only hand-built scow on the river these days."

As we approached the bank, Sally got ready to jump ashore. Our landing technique had improved somewhat by this time, but I had a new idea.

"Instead of trying to hold the boat, maybe we should snub the rope around the nearest tree," I suggested.

"You mean leap out, run up the shore, and tie the rope . . . all in the three seconds it takes for the river to pull the scow from shore?"

"Something like that."

"Show me how it's done," Sally responded with a sly grin.

Taking up the challenge, I scrambled to the front of the scow and loosely coiled the bow rope in my left hand. When I judged we were close enough to the river's edge, I swung one foot out and flung myself towards the shore. It would have been a graceful manoeuvre if the bank hadn't dropped straight down under the water. My foot slid off the edge and I scrambled out of the water on hands and knees, still holding the rope. Both of my boots filled with water. And I thought I'd left that experience behind on the Stikine Trail!

Sally's hoots of laughter echoed across the river as I squished my way through the brush. Just as I reached the nearest tree, the rope went taut and jerked me back down the slope. I managed to hold on, boots skidding across roots and rocks until the scow swung into shore again.

"Great show!" Sally shouted as I finally snubbed the rope around a tree. This technique, which Sally dubbed the "slam-dunk method," would need a little work.

Scow Bay was worth the effort, though. It was a sheltered cove, complete with a creek and sandy beach. Sally and I pitched our tent beside the bay at an ideal campsite in a small clearing.

From that campsite onward, we tried to arrange our overnight stops at interestingly named locations, such as Gold Point and Eagle's Nest Bluff. After all, if someone had taken the time to name the places, they must have stopped there. A few days later we pulled ashore at Shirtwaist Bend, seemingly named for the twists and turns the river took there. Sure enough, we found a level, sheltered spot tucked in the trees.

That night, I pulled out the maps and spread them on the tent floor. Since the first days of our horseback trip, it had been a nightly ritual to plot our progress on the maps. With a fingertip, I traced the twisting blue line of the Yukon River through the green valley and arrived at our location. We had travelled nearly thirty miles, our daily average. I wrote *September 11, Camp #10* on the map and drew an arrow to our position on the river. It was a rewarding way to end the day, to see how far we had travelled.

"Tomorrow we run Five Finger Rapids!" I announced. This was the last major obstacle on the way to Dawson City. Like the Klondikers before us, we slept lightly, thinking of the wild water that lay just around the corner.

THIRTEEN

Rocks and Rapids

Four towering pillars of rock cleaved the river into five channels of turbulent water. Even from a distance, the Five Finger Rapids looked and sounded awesome as whitewater roared through each narrow chasm. As we swept closer I held the oars in the current, slowing our momentum.

"Tell me when to pull ashore," I said, gripping the oars apprehensively. Sally was standing in the stern of the boat, working the sweep and watching for an eddy on the right to pull into. We were anxious to land so we could survey the rapids and choose our course. After all we'd read about the Five Finger Rapids we were taking no chances.

"Now!" she shouted, pushing hard on the sweep. Working together, we steered *Yukon Belle* to the right. As soon as the bow nosed into the slower water of the eddy, the stern swung around, pushed by the faster current.

After tying the scow to boulders, Sally and I climbed to a ridge and looked down on the rapids. From where we stood, the rocks looked like stone pilings from an old bridge. The right-hand passage between the shore and the first pillar was the one the Klondikers had been advised to run. The gap was only the width of a country road, hemmed by vertical walls that squeezed the river into a churning narrows. The waves were biggest at the base of the pillars.

In the early days of the gold rush, stampeders had learned of these rapids through the northern grapevine. As the death toll and accident rate increased, the North-West Mounted Police had posted signs well ahead of the rapids to warn travellers.

"If we aim for the middle of the gap and hang on tight, we should have no problem," I said, feigning confidence.

"Right, no problem," Sally repeated. Neither of us mentioned the standing wave just past the pillar or the rough chop created where the current from the left charged in.

We returned to the scow and checked the lashings that secured our duffle bags. I checked the straps on our gear. Then I poked a finger into the wet caulking in our scow's leaky corner and held it to the wind. Finally, as I inspected the oarlocks, Sally could stand it no longer.

"Are you sure you're not going to check the expiry date on your life jacket?" she asked. Sally didn't have a single procrastinating bone in her body.

"Okay, I'm ready," I replied, and she untied the boat.

I rowed into the current.

As I steered for the middle of the gap, the river caught us in its grip. We were at the point of no return before I could take my second deep breath. The channel between the pillar of rock and shore narrowed. Then, with a deep roar, the water gained even more speed as it entered the chute.

A few backstrokes of the oars and we were into the midst of the rapids. The boat bucked and water splashed over the bow.

"Go to the right!" Sally called out, leaning hard on the sweep as swirling water began pulling us towards the towering pillar. I dipped the oars in and the current almost tore them from my grasp. Levering against the surging water, I pushed with all my strength.

After a roller-coaster ride through the first stretch, a large wave caught *Yukon Belle* under the bow. The wave lifted the scow momentarily, then dropped us into a deep trough of water. We were tossed and bounced from side to side in the choppy waves at the bottom of the chute.

Then, as suddenly as it had started, the ride was over. The current spat us into calm water.

I turned to look back. From here, the rapids looked deceptively tame.

"Let's line the scow upriver and do it again!" I said, gazing at the foaming chasm.

"Be my guest," Sally replied with an expansive swing of her arm. We both knew that it would be impossible to pull the scow upriver against the current.

Not far from Five Finger Rapids, we came to Rink Rapids. This was another tempestuous section that had caused many overloaded or unwary stampeders to swamp. Again, we kept to the right. Afterwards, I wished we had gone left through the more exciting waves. It even occurred to us that it would have added some historical perspective to career into a mid-river rock.

Soon after passing Rink Rapids, the river widened and became dotted with wooded islands. The course of the river had changed since the map had been printed, and choosing the best route was a challenge. This section had been marked "subject to change" on the old river charts. I noticed our map had the same disclaimer.

Over the seasons, shoals and sandbars shrank or grew or changed location. Some disappeared altogether, while others joined nearby islands to block what had been navigable channels. Sally and I scanned the river, assessing the maze of islands and shallow channels.

When in doubt, we kept to the middle of the river. Several times we misjudged where the main current was and found ourselves watching sticks pass us by in the next channel as we languished in a backwater. Then we would heave on the oars until we met the faster current and were on our way again.

On September 14, two weeks after we had set out on Lake Laberge, we arrived at the junction of the Pelly River. Near the junction was the abandoned settlement of Fort Selkirk, a

Nearing Five Finger Rapids

Sally at the sweep

popular stopping point for the stampeders. The old trading post was an intriguing place for us to visit, with history oozing from each musty, dusty old building. Had the rusted whipsaw hanging on a wall been dragged over the Chilkoot Pass? Had it been used to build a scow like ours? Artifacts scattered throughout the settlement were tangible reminders of the river's rich past.

By the time we left Fort Selkirk two days later, the fall colours were at their peak. It was as if an overenthusiastic artist had painted the landscape with broad brush strokes of the brightest hues possible. Whole mountainsides were covered with golden yellow birch trees, and the river was lined with the bright red leaves of fireweed. As Sally and I rounded each bend of the river, we marvelled at the kaleidoscope of colours.

Three days' travel from Fort Selkirk, the White River added its flow to the Yukon River. Tan-coloured water laden with glacial silt coursed in from the west and scoured the hull like sandpaper. At first, we found this sound a bit disturbing, and we wondered if the sand might scour the pitch from the bottom of the boat. To our relief, as the rivers mixed, the scouring sound lessened.

The Yukon River widened as it flowed northwards, and often split into many channels. Choppy waves showed where the water just cleared the boulders and rocks below.

I was gazing at the multicoloured rocks below one afternoon when, without warning, I felt the scow hit bottom.

"We're grounded," Sally informed me, not at all helpfully. Sally shipped the oars and joined me as I jumped overboard. We had to push, pull, and heave the boat over the shoals. It was impossible to pull back against the current so we wrestled it down the shallow water. Sally and I leaped back in as the current caught the scow, hurtling it down the river again.

"Good timing," I said, catching my breath. "Can you imagine chasing our scow down the river if the current had caught it before we climbed in?"

"Speaking of the current, which way should we go now?" Sally asked as we approached another island. I pondered the map, held flat on the seat by two rocks.

"Left."

We had no sooner entered the left channel when *Yukon Belle* came to another grinding halt.

"Oops! Maybe we should have gone right," I said.

When the scow grounded on several more sandbars that day, we understood why the boat trip from Bennett Lake had been hard on partnerships. Klondikers had stuck together on the Chilkoot Pass and endured the trials of whipsawing logs and building their boats. On the river, they began to argue over which channel to follow or where to camp for the night. Even Sally and I grew more edgy each time *Yukon Belle* grounded on shoals.

The discontent was so common that a sandbar near the mouth of the Stewart River was named Split-Up Island. Many stampeders had stopped there, unable to bear their partners any longer. The men divided their gear on the spot and went on alone. There were even reports of some sawing their boat in half.

"Let's pull ashore," Sally declared suddenly when we neared a sandbar at the mouth of the Stewart River.

"So this is it, Split-Up Island," I replied with a laugh, as we steered the scow towards the river bank.

"No such luck! I just thought we could try a little panning," she said, grinning. Until now, the gold pan had served only for baking bannock and bailing out the scow. It was time to try our luck at panning for gold.

Sally panned at the gravel bar for a while, watching for that elusive glint that meant we had struck it rich. I leaned over her shoulder as she swirled the pan.

"Any gold?" I asked.

"No, but a little practice won't hurt. Just think of all the gold waiting for us at Dawson!" Sally replied with that familiar glint in her eye. Even though we didn't find any gold, the sandbar was a pleasant place to take a break from river travel.

Sally and I continued down the river into a cold wind. Although it was only the first day of fall, we were wearing almost every item of our clothing. When I began to stamp my feet on the floorboards, trying to warm my numb toes, Sally suggested that my antics might kick the floorboards loose. It seemed better to endure cold feet.

Over the next days as we drew closer to Dawson City, our conversation turned from gold to food. Although our trail fare was filling and nutritious, it offered no competition to our visions of mouth-watering green salads, sizzling steaks, and slices of chocolate fudge cake.

"Only one more day to real food," I enthused, smacking my lips in anticipation.

On our last night, we set up our tent just upriver from Dawson City. Our arrival was well timed—winter was definitely on its way, marked by flurries of wet snow splattering onto the ground. To ward off the cold, I zipped up my oilskin coat. Then I added a wool scarf that still smelled of horse. Sally and I sat close together by a driftwood campfire as the night grew colder.

"Well, at least we'll make it before freeze-up," Sally said, snuggling even closer to me for warmth.

The next day, we loaded *Yukon Belle* for the last time. It was September 24 and a new part of our adventure lay just a few bends down the river. Once we arrived in Dawson, Sally and I planned to spend the winter near the gold-fields to experience life in the Klondike. Perhaps we'd even fill our trail-worn pan with gold.

We were contemplating what new experiences might lie ahead when we saw a distinctive slide scar on the right bank. We knew immediately what it was, as we'd seen the scarred hillside in many photographs. It had been a beacon for the thousands of travellers who descended the Yukon River during the gold rush.

Sally and I whooped and hollered as loud as any Klondikers had from their rough boats and scows. There, on the bank of the river, was the place we had been struggling towards for months, the place of the great gold rush— Dawson City, Yukon.

Packing up

Riding to the high country

Sally and Mare

Dinner time

A river crossing

146

On the Stikine Trail

Reflections

Ian and Blackie

Boat building

The Yukon Belle

A capable oarsman!

Panning on the Yukon River

Our Klondike home

On the winter trail

Camping at forty below

Thawing with steam

Hand mining with a rocker

Panning for gold

Gold!

A good clean-up of gold

152

FOURTEEN

Klondike Life

I gave one last heave on the oars and *Yukon Belle* turned, sliding up onto the beach at Dawson City. As we tied up our scow among freighter canoes and aluminum skiffs, we noticed that ours was the only hand-built boat in sight. From Klondike photographs, I'd had an image in my mind of the waterfront three-deep with rough boats and row upon row of canvas tents.

Sally and I walked up from the river to Front Street of a quiet, modern-day Dawson. Although the tents were gone, I was surprised that Dawson City hadn't changed much from the old photographs we had seen. Old-style clapboard buildings still lined the river front, and the unpaved streets were still awash with mud.

"And I thought that the streets were paved with gold," Sally mused.

We sloshed through the mud, wearing the rubber boots we'd lived in for the past three weeks. Once we crossed the street, our boots clunked noisily on the wooden boardwalks. The illusion of Klondike times was further enhanced as we exchanged greetings with dancehall performers in their gold rush era costumes and miners in their muddy gumboots.

"This looks like a Wild West town in an old movie," Sally said, referring to a row of false-fronted buildings. Each leaned gregariously against its neighbour and there were few parallel lines in the row. Permafrost had shifted and twisted the buildings, moulding their character. Windows were crooked and door frames were tilted at a jaunty angle.

By early evening, Sally and I were lured towards the music and bright lights of Diamond Tooth Gertie's as readily as any stampeder had been. Then, as now, miners had flocked to the saloons featuring stage shows or extravaganzas of high-kicking dancers and honky-tonk music.

After spending weeks alone in the wilds, our senses were overwhelmed when we entered Diamond Tooth Gertie's. The expansive hall was jammed to capacity with people at card tables, roulette wheels, and slot machines. It was a medley of loud sounds and colourful sights.

"Follow me. I smell food," I said, taking Sally's hand and leading the way to the bar.

Our first priority was to sate our cravings for a fresh salad and a meal that wasn't of the dehydrated variety. Then we turned our attention to the activities around us.

As we overheard snippets of conversations, it became apparent that Dawson City was still a gold-mining town. Groups of men and women discussed mining, their claims, and the results of their efforts.

"My claim on Bonanza pulled in four ounces last week," one bearded miner boasted.

"We're doing pretty well ourselves. I plan to work non-stop on the sluices until the water freezes," his companion replied.

"Well, I think we'll shut down in a couple of weeks," another miner said. "I've done most of the stripping for next season."

Many of the expressions they used were new to us, and we wondered what they meant. Terms like "stripping," "using a monitor," and "doing a clean-up" would take some getting used to. However, the word we did understand was *gold!* Sally's eyes sparkled each time she heard the word; we were closer to the gold and the gold-fields than ever before.

We met one old-timer who told grand tales of prospecting for gold and of finding thumb-sized nuggets. When our conversation turned to the history of the gold rush, we learned that it had taken his father two years to come over the Edmonton Trail. By the time his father had arrived in Dawson there were no claims to be had. He settled anyway and became a partner on a successful claim.

"I'm still working my father's claim," the old-timer added.

I told him of our trip along the Stikine Trail, and we agreed that just getting to the Klondike proved more of an ordeal than many gold-seekers expected.

"No matter how you get here, it's worth the trip," he said. "There's still gold up here. Always will be, even though the snow covers it up in the winter."

As Sally and I chatted with Dawson's denizens, we began to understand that any serious gold mining would have to wait for spring when there was running water to work the sluices. Maybe then we would strike it rich!

A hush fell over the crowd as the lights dimmed and the piano player's voice announced the show was starting shortly. Sally and I found seats near the stage.

We sat back and enjoyed an outstanding performance in the style of the late 1800s. As the piano player pounded a ragtime tune, five dancers kicked their toes high, sending their layered skirts whirling in brilliantly hued, flashing arcs. We were dazzled. So, evidently, were the miners, for during the final number they threw coins at the feet of the dancers.

"What's going on up there?" I asked the waitress.

"That's a tradition from the gold rush," she replied. "Used to be, they'd throw nuggets, but these days poker chips do just as well!"

As we wandered back to our tent pitched on the shore of the river, I reflected on the sights and sounds of our first day in the Klondike.

"I think I'm going to like it here," I stated with great enthusiasm.

"Yeah, but I don't think they'd let you live at Diamond Tooth Gertie's," Sally replied, hooking her arm in mine and moving me along briskly.

She had a point there. Our first task was to find a place to stay for the winter. Although many gold-seekers had endured their first winter in canvas tents like ours, we were not keen to duplicate that part of history. And we certainly didn't want to dismantle our scow and use the planks to build a shelter. We had already pulled *Yukon Belle* above the high-water line where it would be safe for the winter.

We soon discovered that accommodation was as costly and hard to come by as a hundred years earlier. After searching up and down each street in Dawson, we began to wonder if we might have to live in our tent, after all. Then one morning, as we were seeking refuge from the rain in the library, the librarian came to our rescue.

"You should talk with Julie Frisch," she suggested. "Julie has a cabin thirty or forty miles from town that she might let you use."

As it happened, Julie would be visiting the library sometime that afternoon on one of her regular visits. Sally and I waited with fingers crossed.

"If this doesn't work out we can always beg the librarian to let us spend the winter holed up here, reclining on a bookshelf with other authors!" Sally quipped.

We were relieved when we met Julie and her daughter Sylvia and they seemed to be open to the idea of us staying in their cabin.

"It is a special place to us," Julie said. "We don't live there any more but we haven't changed anything for years."

She paused, lost in thought, then continued. "I must tell you there is no power, no running water, and only a wood-burning stove for heat. It's an old log cabin built during the gold rush."

The more she talked about the cabin, the more we were certain it would be perfect. But what could we offer her in exchange for a winter home?

She made it easy for us. "How about cutting a cord of

wood for each month you stay? That can be your rent."

Sally and I were ecstatic. We were short of money, but one thing we wouldn't be short of was time for cutting wood. Winter in the north is a long season.

The next day, Julie took us to the cabin. We followed her inside and she lit a kerosene lamp, which illuminated the room with a friendly, yellow glow. I built a fire in the stove and it was soon crackling cheerfully as it took the chill from the air. Sally and I looked around the cabin and immediately knew that we would feel at home.

"We'd love to stay here," I said to Julie.

Julie smiled. "I had a feeling you would," she replied.

Two days later we moved in with the duffle bags from our scow and the boxes of supplies we had shipped from Whitehorse.

Julie's two-room cabin felt like a Klondike cabin, furnished with all the things we would need for the winter: axes, shovels, water pails, and a comfortable collection of aged furniture. Central heating was supplied by the barrel stove, which sat shoulder to shoulder with an ancient McClary wood-burning range in the front room.

"I look forward to cooking real food in this oven," Sally said, pulling open the door.

"No more pan bread," I agreed, referring to our bannock fried in a pan. "I can't wait for baked goodies, sourdough bread and rolls, and cookies and . . ."

"Guess I'll have to chop a lot of wood if you're doing all that baking," Sally said with a knowing smile.

Cooking here would be easy compared to preparing food on the trail. The front wall was decorated with a medley of pots and pans. In fact, the entire cabin was cluttered with useful objects. It even came with an enamel water jug, an old shaving brush and cup, and a ceramic bed-warmer. We added our well-travelled gold pan to the rustic collection. The pan would serve as a wash basin through the winter.

Some of the liniments and ointments on the shelves looked as though they had been there since the cabin was built. Among them was a green corked bottle labelled

"Pendray's Klondyke Vinegar."

I read the label aloud: "Every person who intends to go to the Klondyke Gold Fields should not forget to take some of Pendray's Concentrated Vinegar with them. It is guaranteed strictly pure, free from any injurious chemicals whatever and twelve times as strong as the ordinary vinegar, and is the best known preventative of scurvy, etcetera, etcetera, in use."

"It sounds like all the other advertisements from gold rush days," Sally replied in amusement. "Ha! Guaranteed scurvy preventatives, a wagon road on the Stikine Trail, and gold-paved streets. It's enough to make a sceptic of any Klondiker."

Our first night in the cabin was luxury compared with the tent we'd been in since June. The cabin was warm and solid. It didn't flap with each gust of wind, although it creaked and groaned now and then as the permafrost heaved underneath. Sally and I also noticed that the cabin came with a family of mice. We didn't mind sharing our new home with these established residents as long as they didn't skitter across our sleeping bag at night.

We wondered what the mice would think of our Klondike fare. Much of our food was similar to that of the stampeders, such as beans, flour, oats, dried fruit, and tea. Because the cabin featured a root cellar where supplies would not freeze, we had stocked up with tinned food, fresh vegetables, and eggs, mostly stored in mouse-proof containers.

"I hadn't really figured on feeding a family of rodents when we were stocking up at the grocery store," Sally said, trying to decide whether the plastic container she was holding could be nibbled through.

"Well, if they munch though those we'll get to relive the winter of 1897, complete with a food shortage," I said, referring to the year that freeze-up had come before stern-wheelers could bring supplies up the Yukon River. Thousands of miners faced starvation, despite their pouches full of gold.

The North-West Mounted Police had posted warning notices: "For those who have not laid in a winter's supply, to remain here longer is to court death from starvation, or at least a certainty of sickness from scurvy and other troubles."

"How would you like to have come all this way, and then realize you had to leave or risk starving?" I asked Sally.

"What a choice. You can't eat gold, but after months on the trail I would find it hard to turn around," Sally replied.

For those who had not found gold, the cost of living in Dawson became unaffordable. By late winter, many people headed out the way they had come, snowshoeing up the Yukon River. They trudged wearily back to the coast, harnessed to sleds laden with just enough provisions for their arduous journey. Luckily, our larder was well stocked.

Our next project was to begin cutting wood. As we walked to a burned-over area near the cabin, I felt the crunch of frozen moss and brittle leaves underfoot. It was early October, and already there was a dusting of snow and the ponds were edged with ice.

"I'll feel better when we have our wood stacked by the cabin," I said to Sally. "I'd rather not be out here in a blizzard at forty below."

The temperature that day was a few degrees below freezing, just right for strenuous work. By the time we had cut down two trees with the old whipsaw we'd found at the cabin, Sally and I were down to shirtsleeves. Once a tree was felled, Sally energetically whacked off the branches with an axe and I sawed the logs into manageable lengths. Together, we hauled them to the cabin. Log by log, our woodpile grew.

After a week of work, I calculated we had stockpiled three cords of wood. We still had to cut an additional two cords for ourselves plus another five for Julie.

"Can you imagine what it would have been like to do all the chores we're doing—and dig for gold, too?" Sally asked, rubbing her aching muscles after a day of woodcutting.

I could see what she meant. In addition to their daily

chores, the miners had put in several hours of toil each day in their search for riches. For those miners, the romance of the gold rush had ended. The reality of life in the Klondike often meant working in sub-zero temperatures each day, then going home to a tent or a low cabin of unbarked green logs. Many miners slept on spruce-bough mattresses and peered out through tiny windows made from glass jars chinked with clay. Each day they went from smoky, cramped tents and cabins to smoky, cramped mine shafts.

Sally and I spent two more weeks cutting, hauling, and stacking firewood. We were inspired to work more quickly as the days became colder and colder.

"It's snowing!" Sally reported the evening of October 26 as she burst into the cabin, accompanied by a blast of cold air. Until now, there had been only a dusting of snow, not enough to blanket the land. Sally shut the door behind her and stamped snow from her boots onto the cabin floor.

"I'm glad we have most of our firewood in. The snow is ankle-deep already." Fortunately we had eight cords of wood stacked near the cabin.

The snowfall reminded us it was time to prepare the cabin for the cold days ahead. First we hunted for the source of the drafts we had been feeling. We could see where the walls had been rechinked again and again with oakum, old flour sacks, and moss. Over the years chinking had fallen out in places. Perhaps it had been loosened by the resident mice as they made entranceways into the cabin.

"The old-timers were pretty resourceful," Sally observed when we discovered pant legs, strips of caribou fur, and tattered socks stuffed in the cracks around the door.

"Care to donate some socks to the project?" I asked.

"I think yours would work better. They're bigger than mine," Sally countered. We settled for moss.

A thick blanket of snow fell gradually, adding to the roof insulation. As the snow became deeper, we banked it high around the walls to keep the cabin warm.

By early November the thin red line in the thermometer

Our Klondike home in winter

Reading by candlelight

hovered around ten degrees Fahrenheit each morning. Although it was still six weeks to the shortest day, the mountains shut off all but a couple of hours of direct sunlight. At nine in the morning it was barely light enough to wander to the outhouse without the help of a candle. By four in the afternoon light was beginning to fade from the white landscape.

With the change of season came the aurora borealis, the northern lights. Our favourite activity each evening was to bundle up in layers of warm clothing and go outside to watch the light show.

One evening, Sally lay beside me in the snow with her head resting on my shoulder. We watched a brilliant green aurora, its skirt hemmed in red, dancing across the sky. A second band of whitish-green light came from above and grew in intensity until the rippling lights merged into one bright glow. Only when the show was over did we notice we were shivering from the cold. We headed back to the warm cabin.

Mid-November brought colder weather, and our thoughts turned to indoor projects. Like Klondikers before us, Sally started her sourdough sponge. The practice of keeping a "sourdough pot," or starter, was widespread during the gold rush and is still used in the bush today. Sourdough had provided the prospectors with a reliable source of leavening that could survive the rugged conditions of the north.

Following an old recipe, Sally mixed one cup of flour, one cup of warm water, and two teaspoons of sugar in an earthenware crock. She whipped the mixture with a wooden spoon until a froth appeared. Then she covered the concoction with a cheesecloth.

"I hope this works," Sally said with some scepticism as she placed the crock in the warm loft.

We peeked into the pot frequently, wondering if the mixture had caught any of the wild organisms supposedly floating in the air. Two days later we had a fermented, bubbly mass of flour, called sponge.

"What does it smell like?" I asked.

"Vinegar with a hint of yeast," Sally said, withdrawing her nose from the bowl. "What do you think?"

"Not too appetizing. Smells like latex paint!" I replied.

"Well, we can't cook with it yet anyway. This is only the starter. We have to add more flour and water first."

I chuckled when I read the recipe. The author suggested not keeping the starter at room temperature with a lid on the container: "This will result in unfortunate accidents as the sourdough will continue working." I wondered if there would be an explosion or if we'd simply wake one morning to find a bubbling, whitish goo creeping across the cabin floor.

Once the starter was ready, Sally stirred in more flour and water. Then she let the mixture sit for a few hours to grow.

That afternoon, sourdough baking in the oven filled the cabin with a tantalizing aroma. We waited impatiently for the first batch. Finally, we tasted our first slices of warm bread. They were rich with a hint of sourness in the flavour and smell. Sally and I smiled with satisfaction as hot butter and blueberry jam dripped down our chins. It was wonderful to be in a warm cabin, cold wind and snow swirling outside, as we munched on sourdough bread!

As I drifted to sleep that night, I listened to the sounds around me: the creak of a log drawing away from a spiked window as the temperature dropped, the whisper of the fire in the barrel stove drawing air, and the faint hiss of snowflakes brushing against a window. The wall beside me was cold and I snuggled closer to Sally under the down sleeping bag. Winter had come to the Klondike.

FIFTEEN

Colder Days

I crawled out of the warm sleeping bag and was jolted awake the moment my feet touched the icy floor. Sally was still asleep so I gritted my teeth and stifled the loud yodel this memorable experience deserved. Before I'd had a chance to pull on my clothes, goose bumps covered my body.

My morning routine began with lighting the wood-burning stove, and I felt warmer as soon as the fire crackled and snapped to life. The stove puffed like a worn-out stampeder climbing the Chilkoot Pass, then roared lustily as air rushed up the chimney. Even the stove-pipes came alive, as if stretching from a night's sleep as the hot air warmed them.

When I opened the door again to throw in several more logs, the flickering firelight cast my shadow in wavering outlines against the log wall.

"Weather check, please," came Sally's muffled voice from deep within the sleeping bag.

I hardly needed to do a weather check. It was eight o'clock and would normally still be dark outside, but bright moonlight filtered through the frosted window.

"It's another cold, clear day," I reported. I scraped a circle of frost from the window-pane and peered out at the thermometer. My report that it was minus thirty Fahrenheit, our coldest day yet, did little to lure Sally out of bed.

Over the next days, the thermometer continued its downward slide. At minus forty the cabin floor was frigid and we wore our felt-lined boots indoors and out. Although we kept the fire fully stoked all day, the cabin was cold except for a circle of warmth around the stove.

Despite the sub-zero temperatures outside, Sally and I were enjoying the slow pace of life in the cabin. With only three hours of sunlight each day, the cabin became the focus of our life: the hub from which we made our forays into the bitter cold to fetch wood, haul water, or visit the outhouse.

We usually stayed in the cabin reading and writing until noon, when the sun finally crested over the hills. Each afternoon we would bundle up in our warmest down-filled clothing to go snowshoeing.

Often our destination was a hill behind the cabin, the only place that received direct sunlight in midwinter. By two o'clock in the afternoon, the sun dipped below the horizon, and on clear days a peach-coloured sunset lingered for a couple of hours. During this afternoon twilight we did our outdoor chores. One of mine was to haul water from the river.

"I'm glad I remembered to cover the water hole with snow last night," I commented to Sally one especially cold afternoon. With a layer of snow insulating the water hole, I would have only a few inches of ice to chop through.

Using a wide chisel attached to a pole, I chipped around the perimeter of the water hole. On my third round I broke through the ice, and water came gushing up. It became difficult to continue chopping without splashing myself, and my boots and wool pants became coated with a sheen of ice. A few more chops and I scooped out the floating ice before lowering a pail into the river.

Climbing the steep, slippery trail from the river was a challenge with a heavy pail in each hand. Each time I slipped, icy water sloshed into my boots.

"There's got to be a better way," I grumbled after another

boot-soaking stumble. When Sally snowshoed past hauling firewood to the cabin, the solution came to me. If I waited for a skim of ice to form on the water in the buckets, I could load the buckets on the toboggan and pull them to the cabin with less effort . . . and dry feet.

Inside the cabin again and warmed with a mug of tea, we went back to writing and sketching. Even during the short hours of daylight, all our work was done by the light of a kerosene lamp. The cabin had been in the shadow of the mountains since early November.

While supper simmered on the stove, we read a page or two of the newspapers hoarded from our last trip to Dawson. Although the news wasn't very up-to-date, it was better than the four-month-old newspapers the Klondikers had kept for their winter reading.

Sally and I put aside one evening a week for laundry. To prepare for this event, I hauled extra buckets of water from the river and balanced them precariously on the wood-burning stove. Our washing machine was an armstrong model, with me supplying the strong arm. With a toilet plunger in hand, I sloshed the clothes in a bucket—one hundred plunges for wash cycle and another hundred for rinse cycle.

After we had wrung out the clothes, I took them outside to freeze-dry. A couple of hours later, Sally went to retrieve our laundry.

"Open the door!" she called. In marched Sally, accompanied by the scarecrow figures of shirts, pants, and grey wool underwear.

"Let's stand them in the corner," I suggested as Sally looked around for a place to put the life-sized forms. We hung them up to finish drying on ropes that criss-crossed the cabin. As the clothes thawed, the smell of wet wool saturated the air.

During the gold rush it had cost almost as much to have shirts laundered and mended as it did to buy new ones. Many miners wore their shirts until they were almost falling off their backs, then threw them away and put on new ones. Fortunately, we never had to resort to that!

"Could you bring up an extra bucket or two?" Sally asked a few days later as I bundled up to fetch water. It was hair-washing night this time, an event we looked forward to once or twice a week.

When the water had warmed on the stove, Sally leaned over a wash-basin while I poured from an enamel jug.

"How's that?" I asked, as I massaged her scalp.

"Feels wonderful," Sally said, almost purring as she enjoyed the simple pleasure of having her hair washed.

Our life in the Klondike involved an interdependence that was very different from the life we had left behind. In addition to becoming accomplished shampooers, we learned to be barbers, doctors, cobblers, and tailors for one another.

Later that evening Sally and I sat by the stove, drying our hair and enjoying each other's company. We played a game of cards to pass the time and munched on raisin bannock. Beside us, the cabin walls boomed as they contracted in the mid-December cold.

By morning, I noticed that the frost had grown thicker on the inside of the windows. At forty below the corner ice patches had joined at the centre, covering each pane of glass. At forty-five below, the nail heads on the front door became white dots of ice. Frost formed in each place we hadn't chinked properly and a rim of white decorated the doorway. Now, at forty-eight below, our "fridge" under the kitchen counter had become a freezer. We pulled the box away from the wall to where it was slightly warmer.

"Iron Grip's shovel handle would have been getting pretty cold about now," Sally said, referring to our mentor from the old photographs. This started me thinking of a story we'd read of how miners measured the temperature years ago. One system involved placing vials filled with mercury, whisky, kerosene, and Perry Davis Pain-Killer outside on a shelf. Mercury solidified at minus forty degrees and whisky at minus fifty-five. Kerosene froze at minus sixty and the painkiller hardened when it was even colder.

"A man going on a journey started with a smile at frozen quicksilver, still went at whisky, hesitated at the kerosene, and dived back into his cabin when the Pain-Killer lay down," one miner had written.

Iron Grip was on our minds a lot these days. We could almost hear him shuffling about our cabin, putting on a pot of tea. I wondered how he would have done living elbow to elbow with some quick-tempered room-mate. We'd heard that irritating habits—such as throat clearing, snoring, humming, or talking too much or too little—were often the start of disagreements. Some men had stopped speaking to each other in November, even though they remained in the same tiny cabin until the spring thaw. Others had drawn a boundary line down the centre of their cabin, each keeping to his own side for the winter. I read of one case where a partner was so disgruntled, he moved out and pitched his tent beside the cabin.

Cabin fever even affected Sally and me on occasion. One day, when the thermometer registered forty-eight below, the cabin seemed too small for two people. I headed outside for the best remedy I knew—a workout at the woodpile.

After half an hour, I returned to the cabin feeling better.

"Welcome back. You look your usual cheerful self again," Sally greeted me. The cabin no longer felt cramped and claustrophobic; now it was warm, cheerful, and cozy.

Sally's cure was to go on snowshoe treks by herself or to spend time at the woodpile as I did. I wondered, though, why she occasionally called out my name as the axe hit the wood. However, our outings had the desired effect; even after a long cold snap in mid-December, we were still best friends.

Just days before Christmas, the temperature warmed to minus thirty for our tree-chopping expedition. Sally and I set off on snowshoes and selected a suitable small spruce tree. We dragged it back to the cabin and, with great ceremony, placed it in our all-purpose gold pan on the table.

That evening, we decorated the tree with colourful strands of wool and shiny metal disks. The disks were Sally's idea: for weeks, she had saved lids from canned goods and painted them with colourful scenes of winter

Laundry day at minus forty

A Klondike Christmas

trees, birds, bows, angels, and stars. My contribution was to wrap a long string of dried beans around the tree.

"Better on the tree than on my plate," I said cheerfully, suggesting a second string of dried-bean decorations. Our Klondike fare was beginning to taste rather bland.

I woke Sally on Christmas morning by serenading her with yuletide songs played on my harmonica. Duffle socks tacked to the wall were bulging with special gifts, and the tree was ringed with parcels that we had picked up on a mid-December outing to Dawson City.

With great willpower, we had set aside the packages from family and friends. Opening them on Christmas day, we found essentials that any snowbound stampeder would have traded great sums of gold for: chocolate bars, candied fruit, chocolate cookies, fruit cake, and more chocolate.

"This chocolate will help keep scurvy at bay," I mumbled through a mouthful of Purdy's cherry creams.

"Chocolate doesn't prevent scurvy," Sally said with a snort.

"Hah! Have I ever had scurvy?" I asked. "And my main calorie source is chocolate." Our families and friends had been well coached on the need for this cold-weather survival food.

After four hours of reading cards and overindulging in chocolate, we dressed for an afternoon walk.

It wasn't long before our face masks turned white, coated with a thick layer of ice crystals. Our eyelashes and toques and the fur ruffs of our parkas also became gilded with white. We hurried back to the cabin, looking forward to warming mugs of hot chocolate.

As I opened the front door, a swirl of cold air swept low across the floor, then condensed into grey wreaths of mist near the stove. The cabin was awash with savoury smells of the simmering rabbit stew and dumplings. Before long, we added the tantalizing aromas of baked sugar cookies and sourdough bread. That evening by the mellow, yellow light of kerosene lamps, we feasted on our special Christmas dinner.

"Here's to the old-timers," I said, raising a mug of hot chocolate in a toast.

"And to the gold they left for us in the creeks," Sally returned.

Once the new year came, Sally and I turned our attention to plans for a snowshoe trek to the gold-fields. One of our goals had been to relive this part of a Klondiker's life, and we calculated that by late February daylight hours would be long enough for travelling. Then we would load camping supplies onto toboggans and snowshoe up Bonanza Creek, past the gold claims of one hundred years ago. If the trip went well, we would continue along the old winter trail another three hundred miles to Whitehorse—just for the adventure of a long winter trek.

We modified two toboggans, adding poles to clip to the hip-belts of our backpacks. I also screwed runners on the base of each six-foot-long toboggan so they would track straight. Finally, I coated the toboggans with wax to help them glide better. We also reinforced our snowshoe harnesses and sewed caribou fur sleeping mats in preparation for the trip.

When those projects were completed we started on the tent. Most travellers in the old days slept under a tarp by a roaring fire or in a tent heated by a small wood-burning stove. Rather than haul such a stove, Sally and I decided to sew a liner for the tent. This second wall would help retain some of the heat provided by our lantern.

To take measurements for the liner, we set up the tent in the back room, stringing it from the rafters and tying out the sides to nails in the log walls. The front room was still cluttered with snowshoes and toboggans needing another coat of wax.

While we were working on the tent, I thought we should run the Coleman stove and lantern outside to calculate how much fuel they consumed per hour in the cold weather. I lit both and set them on the front porch, then went back inside to help Sally measure the tent.

With a pot of tea beside us, we were deeply involved in measurements and calculations when we heard a knock on the front door. This was our first visitor in weeks.

"Come in!" Sally shouted from the tent.

The door opened and our visitor stepped over the two toboggans and a pair of snowshoes lying on the floor.

"We're in the tent," I called, peeking out the door. "Will you join us for tea?"

I saw our visitor, wide-eyed, glance through the window to the roaring stove and lantern outside. Then his gaze wandered across the toboggans and snowshoes inside, and over to the tent pitched in the back room. I thought I heard him mumble something about being bushed.

"Just came to see how you were doing," he said. He declined our invitation for tea in the tent and left after we assured him that we were doing fine.

A few days later, Sally and I were ready to go on a practice run with the toboggans. We loaded each toboggan with several armfuls of firewood, wrapped the logs in a tarp, and secured the bundle with a rope laced over top. I clipped the towing poles onto my hip-belt and leaned forward to break the initial friction of the sled on the snow. To get her sled moving, Sally lunged forward, throwing all her weight against the harness.

We started up the mountain behind our cabin. As we puffed up a long hill, we heard a chain saw running nearby. Someone was cutting firewood. Rounding a bend in the trail, we steamed past the fellow who had visited our cabin a few days earlier.

"Ho there," he called out after turning his chain saw off.

I could see him eyeing our loaded toboggans, probably wondering what we were up to now.

"Going camping?" he asked.

"No, just hauling a load of firewood to the top of the hill and back to the cabin," Sally replied, as if that's what any normal person might do in their spare time.

In true northern fashion, he said nothing about what he thought of our activity. Although, as we leaned into our harnesses to pull away, I thought I heard him mumble something about being *sure* we were bushed.

I looked ahead to Sally, grunting and groaning as she

struggled with her load.

"Maybe we are bushed, after all," I said under my breath. At that moment, even I could see that hauling heavy sleds of firewood up a steep hill for recreation did not seem like a sane thing to be doing.

Even so, Sally and I went on several more practice runs and continued other preparations for our upcoming month-long journey. When planning our camping menus, we decided against the traditional beans, bannock, and bacon because of their weight and cooking time. Instead, we chose our usual nine-grain cereal for breakfast, and lunch would be hard biscuits with salami and cheese, washed down with tea. Suppers would be a choice of freeze-dried chicken glop, dehydrated ground beef slop, or macaroni dinner gluten.

Slop, glop, or gluten. Although the names didn't sound inspiring, we knew from past trips that these were lightweight, nutritious, and sometimes tasty trail meals. We merely had to add a few cups of water and twenty minutes later they would be ready to eat. Our one concession to luxury was a large bag of hot chocolate mix, in spite of its weight. Because we would be pulling sleds, I insisted there would be room to carry the extra bulk of hot chocolate for each night.

"I think we should bring my gold pan too," Sally added as we finished sorting out our gear.

"Any gold will be buried deep under the snow!" I countered. "How about we wait till spring to find your bonanza." Although Sally's gold fever had been dormant for the past few months, it seemed that the symptoms were reappearing as we planned our trip from Dawson to the gold-fields.

By mid-February our toboggans were packed and ready to go and we waited impatiently for the minus forty-five degree weather to moderate. Sally and I looked forward to getting a sense of what it had been like for the Klondikers to travel during winter. Besides, cabin fever was starting to set in. Nothing would make a small cabin more attractive than a few weeks in our tent at sub-zero temperatures.

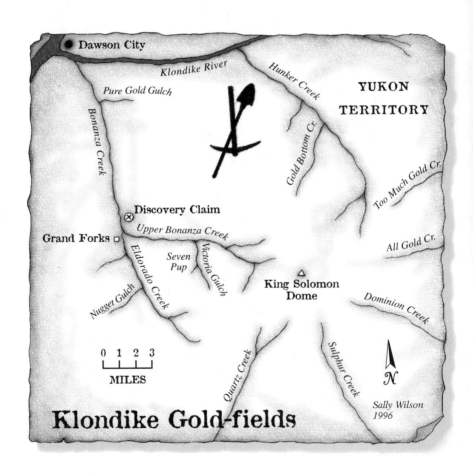

Dawson City

Klondike River

Pure Gold Gulch

Hunker Creek

YUKON
TERRITORY

Bonanza Creek

Gold Bottom Cr.

Too Much Gold Cr.

Discovery Claim

Upper Bonanza Creek

Grand Forks

All Gold Cr.

Eldorado Creek

Seven
Pup

Victoria Gulch

King Solomon
Dome

Dominion Creek

Nugget Gulch

0 1 2 3

MILES

Quartz Creek

Sulphur Creek

N

Sally Wilson
1996

Klondike Gold-fields

SIXTEEN

By Snowshoe and Sled

Kicking the tips of our snowshoes forward, Sally and I moved through deep snow along the Klondike River towards the gold-fields. Our loaded toboggans followed us obediently, pushing a wave of white ahead of them. It was February 28 and we had started on our journey despite the temperature, which still hovered near minus thirty degrees.

With each step, we strained against our sled loads of tent and liner, camp equipment, trail food, and sleeping gear. Our backpacks bulged with extra clothes and items we might need during the day.

There were no other characters hauling toboggans up the river, although a century ago Sally and I would have been jostling for trail space with hundreds of Klondikers hauling sleds. Some would have been coming into Dawson for supplies, or for companionship in the bars. Others might have been returning to their claims with a sled loaded with grub, or perhaps heading back with a hangover, an empty gold poke, and an empty backpack.

Sally and I continued along the river, then turned south up the Bonanza Creek valley. The snow-filled depression of Bonanza Creek looked insignificant, barely four paces wide. I found it hard to believe that it was the source of so much gold. Several claims had yielded one million dollars' worth of the yellow metal—when gold was only sixteen dollars a troy ounce!

Several names on the map told of golden dreams and riches that had been found in the area: Pure Gold Gulch, Eldorado Creek, Nugget Gulch, Ready Bullion Gulch, and Gold Bottom Creek. We snowshoed on, eager to visit these places.

On our second day Sally and I came to the site where George Carmack, with Skookum Jim and Tagish Charlie, had made the discovery that sparked the Klondike gold rush. On August 16, 1896, the three had been exploring Rabbit Creek when they found gold lying between the flaky slabs of rock, "like cheese in a sandwich."

They staked their claim, and the creek was soon renamed "Bonanza." Up and down the Yukon River the news spread like wildfire. Prospectors who had been searching along the Yukon River for years poured into the area. In less than two weeks Bonanza Creek had been completely staked.

"Just think, there might be gold right under our snowshoes," Sally said. "This is where the Klondikers found their millions!" I thought she was going to grab the shovel from my toboggan and start digging right on the spot.

Sally and I decided to camp by the plot of ground where Carmack's discovery had indirectly inspired our own journey to the Klondike. The sun had already dipped behind the hills as we began to set up camp beside a sheltering grove of willows. While Sally stamped down a tent platform with her snowshoes, I gathered firewood for a campfire.

After lighting the fire, I scooped up a pot of snow and suspended it over the flames. Before long, we had a pot of water, complete with spruce needles and other debris that had been in the snow. A strong brew of tea hid the distinctive snowmelt flavour.

"Tired?" I asked as I topped up Sally's mug.

"A bit," Sally admitted. She smiled wearily and sipped her

tea. "Nothing a warm sleeping bag and a good night's rest won't fix, though."

I took that as my cue to start setting up our accommodation for the night. Sally held the tent poles upright while I tied out each corner rope to snowshoes jammed into the snow. Once it was set up, the tent didn't look nearly as cozy as it had when pitched in the cabin. The thin canvas walls now looked less than adequate as shelter against the frigid night.

It wasn't long before we were settled in our canvas home and supper was cooking on the camp stove. Lantern-light cast a cheerful glow on the walls. As I sat with a mug of soup warming my cold hands, I was surprised how warm the tent seemed. The combined heat of the stove and our Coleman lantern made it at least twenty degrees warmer inside the canvas walls than it was outside.

As we burrowed into our zipped-together sleeping bags, Sally and I talked about our first day on the trail.

"I hadn't realized it would be so difficult to haul those sleds," Sally said.

I was sympathetic. Rubbing her tired shoulders, I reminded her of an old guidebook we'd read in Dawson that claimed toboggans would "slide over the snow with scarcely a tugging reminder." This statement was just another of the many exaggerations the Klondike guidebooks had passed on. Normally, Sally would have led, setting a brisk pace. Today she had dragged behind, struggling with her load and stopping to rest frequently.

"Scarcely a tugging reminder . . . ha!" I said, laughing out loud. Sally joined me. It wasn't a punch line that would cause many people to laugh, but in our tired state we began giggling uncontrollably.

"Imagine what it must have been like for the miners, hauling load after load of supplies up this route," I added on a more serious note.

"Mmm," came Sally's reply, just before her deep breathing told me she had fallen asleep. I don't think she was much interested in stories about old miners at that point.

I turned off the lantern and nestled down into the sleeping bag. My interior heater, well-stoked with a filling supper, began to warm the bag. Finally I relaxed and stretched out, then fell into the deep sleep that a day of strenuous outdoor activity brings.

We rolled out of the warmth of the down-filled bag as diffused daylight illuminated the tent. Without looking at my watch, which was still buried somewhere in the sleeping bag, I guessed it was about nine o'clock. Dressing hurriedly in the icy tent, we pulled on layer upon layer of woollen clothes.

"Hey!" I complained when Sally brushed against the tendrils of frost that hung from the ceiling, showering me with ice crystals.

"I'll wait here until you've finished dressing," I said, flopping back into the bag. There wasn't room for both of us to dress in bulky clothing without elbows and knees ending up in each other's ribs and ears.

Soon after leaving camp, we came to Cheechako Hill. When Oliver Millet, a newcomer, or "cheechako," had learned that the valley bottom was completely staked, he decided to try his luck on the hillsides. His theory was that a bench above the valley might be where Bonanza Creek had flowed long ago.

Old-timers thought that gold was found only in the valley bottoms and they laughed at the ignorance of this cheechako. Their laughter turned to amazement when Millet found the ancient gold-rich channel of Bonanza Creek. His discovery claim yielded gold worth more than half a million dollars.

Farther on, at the junction of Eldorado Creek, we snowshoed over the old townsite of Grand Forks. A hundred years ago this had been a bustling community of three thousand people. Now, the only visible remains were one or two skeletons of buildings poking up through the snow.

From there, Sally and I turned onto Upper Bonanza Creek. Our progress was unbearably slow. The trail led up an unrelenting grade, and fresh snow delivered throughout the day slowed our progress even more.

To break the monotony, I slipped into a routine. I took fifty steps, then paused. After fifty more I hitched up the pack belt, which had worked its way down my hips. Another fifty and I rested for a minute.

Every hour or so we took a packs-off rest stop to sip hot tea from our thermos and nibble some trail food. At our midday rest stop I poured the last drops of tea into the mug.

"Trade you a piece of chocolate for an extra gulp of tea," Sally bargained. It was an enticing offer, but I was as thirsty as she was. Breathing the cold, dry air had a way of sucking away the four cups of liquid we drank each morning. We had one gulp each and settled for hard candies to quench our thirst.

We hooked the tug poles to the straps on our hip-belts then continued up the trail. There were no sounds except our rhythmic breathing and the muffled shuffle of our snowshoes on the snow. If we had been here in the winter of 1898 we would have heard the sounds of picks thudding into the frozen ground and shovels scraping against the gravel. The hillside would have echoed with the creaking of windlasses as the miners hoisted buckets of dirt from their shafts. Miners at their cabins would have added the sounds of sawing logs and splitting firewood to the din. I paused and looked across the valley, visualizing the past, until the rusty-hinge croak of a raven brought me back to the present.

Sally and I camped that night near Carmack Fork, where a narrow valley intersected with Upper Bonanza Creek. A century ago, we could have stopped at the Colorado roadhouse for a drink at the bar or a place to sleep. In fact, we could have stopped at many such establishments along the way. According to Tappan Adney, "wherever there was a tent and a bottle of whisky, a saloon sprang up."

As we set up our meagre canvas shelter for the night, I understood why there had been many roadhouses. After a day on the trail, travellers would gladly have traded some of

Hauling a toboggan

Winter camp

their hard-earned gold for a warm place to stay.

"I would certainly pay for a roadhouse bed that wasn't hollowed out in the snow," I commented to Sally.

"I could sing a song for a roadhouse atmosphere," she offered. Somehow it wouldn't have been the same. Even so, the warmth of the Coleman lantern was a welcome luxury after our day outdoors.

The next morning was especially cold. An hour after we started on the trail, the wind picked up. With the wind-chill factor, the temperature dropped to minus forty and our exposed faces became taut and numb. Even our hands and feet became cold, despite wearing three layers of mitts and the warmest felt liners in our boots. The frigid air bit at our lungs with each laboured breath.

Looking back, I saw that Sally's eyebrows, cheeks, and the ruff of her hood were coated with white rime. I pulled my toboggan to one side so she could snowshoe up beside me.

"Thanks, partner," Sally said, smiling as I warmed a white frost-nipped patch on her cheek with my bare hand. After that we made a point of checking each other's face for frostbite every few minutes.

By lunch time, despite chugging up a steady grade, our hands and feet were still numb with cold.

"How about a fire?" Sally suggested as she slapped her hands together to restore circulation. I nodded my agreement and we found a windbreak formed by a stand of spruce trees. We collected dry twigs and branches. Within minutes we were thawing our icy fingers over the flames of a crackling campfire.

Sally and I huddled as close to the heat as we dared, watching for sparks that might burn holes in our parkas. I pondered the miracle of fire as my hands began that painful, stinging sensation of returning to life.

Warmed by the fire and fueled with slices of salami and cheese, we continued up the hill. Each time I looked at Sally, she was puffing in the cold air like a steam engine.

By early the next afternoon we began traversing a long

ridge that offered a striking view of King Solomon Dome. To the north, a row of rugged peaks thrust skyward, clean-edged and white against blue. These were the Ogilvie Mountains. In the broad valley we could see the snaking indentation of the North Klondike River. Somewhere, hidden in the trees, was our winter cabin.

"Beautiful!" I puffed. I leaned into my harness so the toboggan wouldn't slide back down the hill.

"Mmmph," Sally responded. She looked ready to collapse. In fact, Sally was having trouble on almost every hill, and we had been climbing steadily for four days. In that time, we had gained more than three thousand feet in elevation.

On one hill, Sally stalled out completely. Her snowshoes were stuck out sideways as she leaned forward to counter the pull of the toboggan.

"Lean forward MORE!" I encouraged.

"But my nose is almost touching the snow!" Sally protested. No matter how much she leaned into her harness, the weight against her hip-belt pulled her back down the hill. With much grunting and groaning and slipping and sliding she struggled up the slope, two steps forward and one backward.

When Sally stopped to take another rest, I began to wonder if I had mistakenly switched sleds that morning. The loads were wrapped in the same trail-worn tarps that had covered our pack-boxes and been a sail for our scow. Our sleds looked identical, but mine was considerably heavier.

"Uh, Sally," I began cautiously, not quite sure how to broach the topic. "I think you might be pulling my sled."

"What?" she asked, steam rising from her parka. With a groan, she collapsed into the snow. I unhooked my tug straps and compared the weights of the sleds. Sally did not find it nearly as amusing as I did when we discovered that she had hauled the heaviest toboggan up the steepest hill.

All afternoon, Sally and I continued up the steep grade. My pace was slower now. Leaning forward with my head down, I had ample opportunity to study the trail under my snowshoes. Especially cold temperatures the night before had caused a thick layer of hoarfrost to coat every bush and every twig. When I snowshoed across them, they flew upward then landed with a tinkle. I looked towards the sun and saw millions of crystals floating in the air, sparkling brilliantly in the sun's rays.

We felt encouraged as we neared the summit of King Solomon Dome, the highest point of our planned journey.

"This was worth the climb. Look how far we've come," Sally enthused. I looked at her in surprise. Was this the same person who had been groaning up the steep hills? This was more like Sally, climbing a hill just for the view. Wordlessly, I gave her a big hug. The climb was forgotten as we gazed over the panorama of mountains and sky.

Behind us, Upper Bonanza Creek wound down the valley towards Dawson. Other gold-bearing creeks emanated like spokes of a wheel from the Dome. Looking around us, we could see the valleys of Bonanza, Hunker, Dominion, Sulphur, and Quartz Creeks.

"This view is so terrific, I think we should make camp right here," I said, looking around for a sheltered spot for the tent. Sally quickly unhooked her sled and dropped her pack in agreement.

"I guess you'll be up first tomorrow morning to catch the sunrise," Sally said later.

"I might just do that," I said. Sally knew me well. One of the few things that could make me volunteer to get up first was a photo opportunity.

At daybreak I bundled up in my warmest clothes and headed outside. I was rewarded with a breathtaking sunrise that burst over the horizon minutes after I had set up the camera. The sun's rays brushed a pink glow onto the snow, contrasting with deep purple shadows in each hollow. After taking several photographs, I dived back into the warmth of the tent for breakfast.

"Seeing as you're dressed for the job, I'll let you do the toboggans again," Sally said. The task of digging out the snowshoes and preparing the sleds was cold work. I did this job most mornings anyway, because my hands never became as cold as Sally's.

When Sally sent a stream of bags flying out the tent door, it was my cue to start taking the tent down. By the time I had untied the ropes Sally came out to help.

"It looks as if we could have left the tent poles behind to save weight," Sally commented, chuckling. The tent stood in place, unsupported by any ropes or poles. The canvas was frozen solid with the moisture from steaming pots and our breaths that had condensed on the walls.

Sally and I wrestled the frozen form of the tent to the ground, and with hollers that would have scared away any onlookers, we jumped on the stiff canvas to make it bend. After each fold we attacked the tent again to flatten the package into a manageable size to fit on my toboggan.

We had an easier day winding down the Sulphur Creek valley, the weight of our sleds pushing us downhill. For the first time on our journey, the sleds indeed followed with "barely a tugging reminder." It was a pleasant break from the drudgery of hauling them to the summit.

In camp that night, Sally voiced what I had been thinking. "We have a good idea what hauling sleds up and down mountains is all about," Sally said. "I'd like to see what the river route is like."

Sally and I usually arrive at the same conclusions, and I readily agreed with her suggestion. We had reached the outer limit of the richest Klondike claims, and there was not much to see in the way of history by continuing over the mountain route to Whitehorse. We decided to retrace our trail back towards Dawson and continue our trip to Whitehorse along the Yukon River route.

Two days later, on our way down Upper Bonanza Creek, we stopped at an old cabin beside the trail. It had been hand-hewn with an axe long ago, and moss oozed from between each log. Propped up against the wall was a battered shovel and a well-worn pickaxe. A gold pan, rusted through on one side, was nailed to the wall. Even the padlock on the door looked like a museum piece.

"I wonder what relics are buried under the snow," I mused. Perhaps beneath my snowshoes lay an old sluicebox or a flume from gold rush days.

As we finished exploring around the cabin I felt a snowflake land softly on my cheek. I looked up through the trees and saw dark clouds flowing down the valley, bringing a snowstorm our way. A clearing beside the cabin looked like an ideal place to set up camp and wait out the coming storm.

It was a magical evening as we sat outside the tent eating supper. Hanging in a tree, the lantern cast long, finger-like shadows from the branches onto the snow. The sparks from our campfire darted into the dark sky and the flames cast an orange glow across the snow. Beyond the glow, there were only shadows and snowflakes softly sifting down from the clouds.

"I feel a strong sense of history here," Sally said, looking over to the dark form of the cabin. "Perhaps Iron Grip tromped by here long ago in his search for gold."

We sat quietly, and it seemed we could hear the thud of an axe splitting wood, like an echo from the past. Perhaps there still were miners on the creeks, moiling for gold in their shafts through the winter months.

SEVENTEEN

Bonanza Creek

Like a spirit from Klondike past, a miner materialized out of a swirling snowstorm, his form barely discernible in the diffused light of early morning. His leather boots squeaked on the dry snow and the legs of his canvas pants swished against each other as he walked towards us. Two battered metal pails in his right hand clanged together with each step. I rubbed my eyes, wondering if this apparition could be a result of dreaming too much about the gold rush during the night.

We must have looked almost as peculiar to him: two travellers with toboggans, beside an old-style canvas tent held up by snowshoes. But if he thought we were an odd sight, he didn't let on.

"Hi, strangers. Not many travellers up this way these days," he said. The miner spoke. He was indeed real!

We soon learned that Jerry Bryde had a claim nearby. He was in his early forties and had been hand mining in the area for almost fifteen years. His tanned features spoke of years spent living outdoors. A broad smile and sparkling blue eyes spoke of a contentment with his chosen way of life.

"I just came down to get washing water from the spring," he said. "Why don't you come up and visit?"

We jumped at the opportunity to spend time with a miner and learn about gold mining. It was an offer we couldn't refuse! Jerry went on ahead, leaving us to pack up camp. Within minutes Sally and I followed his trail, climbing steadily up Victoria Gulch.

After an hour of climbing, we heard the ring of an axe echo across the valley.

"That must be the sound we heard last night," I said as we neared the crest of the hill. Then we smelled smoke from a wood fire. Around the next bend in the trail, we came to an appealing little cabin with a line of grey smoke curling out of the chimney. This was Jerry's home.

Jerry was in the yard to greet us. He led the way to his cabin, his arms full of firewood.

"Tea's on. Come on in," he said, hospitably.

We left our boots on the porch after noticing the sign: "Boots here or you'll be sentenced to one day of hard labour on Seven Pup."

Sally and I perched on the edge of the bed while Jerry sat on a wooden chair across the room. There was less than an arm's length between us in the narrow cabin.

As we sat sipping tea, I had an opportunity to study Jerry. His sinewy body, earthy language, and whiskered face fit the image of a sourdough, and his features were moulded from a life of mining. Years of swinging a pick had given him broad shoulders and muscled forearms. His hands were calloused from handling a shovel and chapped from panning in icy water.

"Like my haircut?" Jerry asked, turning his head so we could view it from all angles. "I cut it myself yesterday."

I didn't reply. His beard was neatly cropped, but his hair looked as if someone had taken a machete to it.

"Well, I don't have a mirror, so I'll take your word that it looks great!" he said with a grin. I laughed and realized his sense of humour matched ours.

We looked around the room; this was definitely a miner's

cabin. A tub of water with a gold pan resting in it occupied the centre of the room. Each window-sill was crowded with magnifying loupes, chunks of quartz with flecks of gold, and other rock samples. Gold pans of all sizes were on countertops, on the floor, and on the warming tray of Jerry's stove. The smallest pans were used as ash trays, while some of the larger ones contained small mounds of dull yellow metal. A set of brass scales hung on the wall.

Despite the clutter, the cabin was spotless. The room was much longer than it was wide, and a cupboard with a fold-out flap served as the larder and kitchen. The small room was easily heated with an old-style wood-burning range, which featured a large oven and a hot water tank.

"The oven works well. I bake all my own bread," Jerry commented when he saw me looking over the stove.

Judging by the heat the wood-burning range was belting out, I had no doubt the oven worked well. Unused to warm rooms, Sally and I stripped off layer after layer until we were down to our long underwear. We settled in for a good sweat.

While we sipped mugs of tea poured from an enamel pot, Jerry told us about his mining life. He talked about how he had come north looking for a job and ended up working for a miner in the Klondike. After learning what he could about placer mining, he ventured out on his own. He has been working various claims in the area ever since.

Jerry continued his story. "I've settled in here for a while. There's enough gold on that hill to keep me busy hand mining for years," he said pointing out the window.

"You might say all my assets are frozen!" he added, laughing heartily at his joke.

"People think I'm crazy to spend winters up here, but I love it. I have so many projects to work on and piles of books to read. I save all my magazines to read in the winter and nobody comes up to bother me. They can't get here!" he added with a chuckle.

"But I do like visitors," he quickly assured us, when Sally pointed out that we had managed to climb up the steep trail to his cabin.

The afternoon passed too quickly and we were thrilled to be invited to visit again the following morning. Sally and I headed down the hill while there was just enough light to see the trail.

In the morning, dressed in our warmest clothes, we followed Jerry on a tour of his claims. He showed us where he'd been working the past few weeks.

"There are two veins of quartz running through my claims. Up here, there's usually gold associated with quartz, so I've been digging pits to try and plot exactly where the quartz runs," he explained.

Jerry talked as he walked, and we followed him along a well-packed trail leading from pit to pit. He told us there were two sources of gold on his claims: the quartz veins cutting through his area, and the surface material that had migrated downslope from quartz veins that cut through the Lone Star claim above Seven Pup.

"I keep three or four fires burning at the same time," Jerry said when I caught up to him at the next pit. "When a fire has gone out after burning for five or six hours, I can dig away the thawed soil."

"How deep can you dig each time?" Sally asked.

"Not even a shovel's depth. It takes many days to dig a six-foot test pit. I keep busy going back and forth all day, digging, burning, and digging."

While we toured the claim, it struck me how similar Jerry's life was to that of miners one hundred years ago. We had read about Klondike miners' lives during the gold rush but never expected to meet someone who was actually living that way.

Seeing Jerry's operation reminded me of accounts I had read of gold-seekers labouring in their pits during the long, cold winter. Each day, they added to the mound of dirt and gravel outside their cabins. Every miner dreamed of spring, when the streams would run again and there would be enough water for sluicing. Only then would they learn if they were still poor or if they had struck it rich. Some miners literally sat on a fortune in gold throughout the winter.

"How did the first miners know where to dig?" I asked.

"They panned the dirt as they went, then dug in the direction that showed the most colours."

Back at the cabin, Jerry put more logs into the stove and an hour later we had a mug of hot chocolate. And so life went on in a cabin in the north. Time meant little, and we talked until it was nearly dark again.

"I love this life, these quiet winters balanced with hectic, eighteen-hour days during the summer when I just give 'er," Jerry said.

Another day with Jerry had passed quickly and it was time for us to return to our camp. Jerry suggested we stay for a few days and offered us the use of the old cabin in the valley where we'd left our tent. We quickly accepted, looking forward to a warm place to stay.

By the light of the stars and the northern lights, Sally and I descended the steep trail to the valley. Once our eyes became used to the dark, we could just make out a faint shadow outlining one side of the trail. Each time I stepped off the hard-packed trail, I floundered in soft, knee-deep snow.

I joined Sally where she had stopped in a clearing. Together we stood watching comets streaking across the black sky and cutting through the glowing northern lights. When the cold finally seeped through the folds of our down-filled jackets, we started down the hill again.

Sally and I spent a comfortable night sharing the warm log cabin with a family of squirrels. We arrived back at Jerry's place mid-morning with the first rays of sun. Inside, we found him surrounded by a collection of sample bags strewn across the floor. He was preparing to pan out the contents of each bag to see if there was any gold.

"I'll show you where this soil came from. This winter I built fires and dug pits all along the ridge. These are the samples from the pits," he said, running his finger along the map tacked on the wall.

The map showed a layout of the region, which was

divided into claims on every valley and gully. Jerry's claims, outlined in red, were at the top of Victoria Gulch. Jerry explained the numbering system on the maps. On each watershed, the claims were numbered from the discovery claim, the first claim registered on that creek. The claims were numbered in order from One Above Discovery, Two Above, and so on. Downstream they were similarly called One Below, Two Below, and so on down the valley.

"Why was this area called Seven Pup, then?" Sally asked.

Referring to the map again, he explained that the watershed was Upper Bonanza Creek. Tributaries flowing into watersheds are called gulches. Water systems flowing into the gulches are known as pups.

"This pup flows into claim number seven on Victoria Gulch so it's called Seven Pup," he said.

"I don't name claims after girlfriends as some people do. I name my claims after exotic cars." Jerry told us that the claim at his cabin was called "Countach." Sally and I looked more closely at the map; the name of each claim now meant more to us than they had before.

On the map, Jerry pointed out the Lone Star claim that was above Seven Pup. It was situated on one of the gold-bearing faults, called shear zones, which extend for miles across the Klondike region. Later, we learned something that the Klondikers would have traded a poke of gold to know: many of the gold-bearing shear zones parallel a landform called the Tintina Trench, which runs the length of the continent.

Sally and I were so intrigued by gold and Jerry's stories that we put our snowshoe trip on hold and decided to visit Seven Pup for as long as we were welcome. For the next week we climbed the hill every morning.

Jerry put us to work hand mining, and we started by burning a prospecting pit. While Sally cleared away a large area of snow, I cut firewood with a bow saw. After the fire was started, we kept the flames burning for six hours, adding more and more wood throughout the day. We were kept busy sawing and hauling wood and tending the fire.

Finally, we began to remove the thawed earth. The top layer of soil was soft enough to dig through, but below that I had to work with the pickaxe to gain another inch or two. That was all. We had only removed six inches of earth after our six-hour fire. At this rate it would take a long time to reach bedrock!

"Up here, anyone could be a gold miner. It was a poor man's chance at finding a fortune," Jerry said. "All you needed was a pick, shovel, a big fire, and a strong back."

Well, we had all of those. I decided one more thing was required: strong motivation.

Jerry explained that the permafrost was both a curse and a blessing for hand-miners. Although it was nearly impossible to dig through, the frozen earth meant there was little chance of a shaft or tunnel caving in.

As we worked in our pit the next day, Jerry came by to check on our progress.

"Not quite ready for a bucket and windlass yet," he chuckled. Our hole was only three spade-depths beneath the surface.

Jerry told us that after prospectors reached bedrock, they began "drifting." They built a fire at the side of the shaft where they thought the richest pay dirt would be. Then they kept thawing and shovelling and hauling out the muck until they found gold—or gave up.

"If you guys dig a deep pit, maybe I'll let you see what drifting is all about," Jerry said with a mischievous grin.

"There must be an easier way!" Sally groaned, heaving another shovelful of dirt from the test pit.

"Actually, there is," Jerry said. "I just wanted you to see what it was like to work like a real hand-miner first!"

EIGHTEEN

Searching for Gold

The next morning we found Jerry working on a black cylindrical contraption that stood taller than him. Valves, gauges, pipes, and hoses sprouted from every side. The object sat on a square box, looking like a rocket ready for liftoff.

Jerry explained that it was a steam thawing machine from the early 1900s. "It's a tough job digging pits by burning, so I'm going to get my steam boiler working," he said.

"Basically, a fire in the box heats water to steam, and the steam comes down the hose to this metal shaft," he continued, pointing to a long pipe. "Then the steam does the work of thawing the ground."

Jerry told us that steam thawing was invented during the gold rush by an Eldorado Creek miner named Clarence Berry. Berry had noticed that the steam from a boiler hose had bored a hole in the frozen ground. He attached the hose to a rifle barrel and found that his new "steam point" thawed the ground more efficiently than burning with open fires. And so the first steam point was put into use.

"If you help me get it ready and cut a couple of cords of wood, I'll show you how it works," Jerry suggested.

We leaped to the task.

"Oh, by the way," he added, "we also have to drag the boiler up that hill so I can dig some test pits." I began to wonder about our timing.

We left Jerry to work on the machine while we climbed the hill to cut down some trees. Once Sally and I had cut and stacked an impressive-looking pile of wood, we began shovelling snow from the area where the pit would be.

It took the combined muscle power of all three of us to haul the unwieldy boiler up the hill on a sled. We wrestled the pieces from the sled, then Jerry and I worked with pipe wrenches to assemble the boiler. Sally continued bringing the rest of the paraphernalia we would need to start the project: pails for melting snow, a hand pump, hoses, a pick, and a shovel.

We set the firebox on a platform of poles, then installed the boiler on top. Once the smokestack was in place, the entire rig, perched on the side of the hill, looked as if it might topple over.

"I love the challenge of getting old equipment like this running again," Jerry said as we tightened the pipe fittings. "I didn't buy any parts but scrounged what I needed. That's what the old-timers would have done."

While Jerry tinkered with the pressure release valve, Sally and I connected a long rubber hose from a pipe at the top of the boiler to the steam point. This shoulder-high metal pipe was the working end of the machine; it would be used for thawing the frozen ground.

"Let's warm up the boiler before pumping the water in," Jerry suggested.

Sally prepared the firebox with kindling and lit a match. Smoke puffed from the smokestack, and the entire boiler began ticking and groaning as it heated up. Minutes later, flames burst out of each crack in the firebox of the ancient contraption.

Using a hand pump of the same vintage as the boiler, we transferred water from a pail into the boiler. Jerry told us that we would have to calculate how much to stoke the fire in relation to how much water was in the tank. He set the metal pail on a corner of the firebox so we could keep it filled with snow to melt for water.

Finally, all the gauges and valves and dials were working to Jerry's satisfaction.

"Keep a close eye on the pressure gauge," Jerry advised. "I've learned that twenty to forty pounds is enough. When a hose blows at a hundred pounds it gets pretty exciting!" After that, we watched the dial as if it was attached to a load of dynamite.

Although the air temperature that day hovered around minus twenty-five, it took only fifteen minutes for pressure to build in the boiler.

"This is a sweetheart," Jerry said running a hand along the upper body of the boiler. I knew the heat felt good on his hands after working barehanded with the wrenches.

Jerry glanced at the pressure gauge and announced, "Steam's up!" He passed me the steam point then opened a valve to release the steam down the hose.

"Just push it gently into the ground," he shouted over the hiss of steam. "The point will slide in as it thaws the frozen dirt."

After a few minutes, I pulled the steam point out of the hole to see how it was working. With a deafening hiss, pressurized steam burst out of the pipe and instantly enveloped me in a cloud of white vapour. Yikes! I jammed the point back into the ground.

After showing Sally how to control the steam pressure, Jerry left us to work alone. That way, he said, we could learn for ourselves what life on the creeks had been like years ago. A couple of hours later, Jerry returned to check on our progress.

"Looks good," he said. "Let's take a break."

The three of us stopped for a mug of tea from a thermos, but the pressure building up in the boiler cut our rest short. Jerry left again to tend the fires he was burning in several pits nearby.

In the low afternoon light, the boiler appeared to be alive.

Sally and Jerry at the steam boiler

Steam thawing

It hissed loudly, and from deep within, water gurgled as if the boiler had indigestion. With a loud belch, smoke and sparks spewed skyward from the chimney. Its breath came in short gasps as air was sucked into the firebox.

With a roar, steam exploded from the point, spraying me with mud each time I lifted the point to start a new hole. Sally said I was often lost to her sight, enveloped by a thick cloud of steam.

"How's the pressure?" I called out to Sally, when the steam point stopped hissing.

"It's at ten pounds, but I've just stoked the fire," she shouted back. It would take practice to become efficient. We had to learn the right balance of wood and water to maintain the pressure we needed. I stuck the steam point back into the hole and turned a tap, cutting off the steam to the point to give the pressure a chance to build.

I joined Sally by the warm firebox to wait. Soon the needle of the gauge had climbed to forty, then fifty pounds of pressure. I scrambled back down to the pit.

"It's up to eighty pounds," Sally shouted moments later. "Open the valve!"

"I did, but nothing's coming out of the point."

Sally closed the draft to the firebox to decrease the heat to the boiler. In a state of nervous anticipation, we watched the gauge, wondering when the boiler might reach blast-off pressure. Meanwhile, I tried to thaw the point in the smokestack. We assumed the point was blocked with ice.

"It's still blocked. Maybe the point isn't frozen after all. The metal feels hot on my hands."

"I'll get Jerry," Sally announced, setting off at a run down the hill.

As an afterthought, I tightened the square nut locking the hose to the point. I decided that this was a place where the contraption might blow apart under pressure; I had no desire to have my face steam-cleaned.

Minutes later, Jerry came to the rescue.

"I bet I know what the problem is. The point is blocked with mud. It's happened to me a few times."

Jerry explained that if we turned off the valve while the steam point was in the ground, the resulting vacuum would suck up dirt and block the hole. Jerry checked that the valve leading to the point was fully closed. Then he stood to one side and cautiously poked a piece of wire into the end of the steam point. Out blasted the offending material: a plug of mud and grit.

While we waited for the fire to regain momentum, we nestled comfortably in a snowbank, drinking tea and talking about a miner's life.

It wasn't long before we had full pressure again. As he left, Jerry looked over his shoulder with a grin. "The old-timers wouldn't have taken breaks like that," he said.

What a slave driver! But Sally and I loved every minute of it. Where else could we have this kind of hands-on mining experience?

I swung the pickaxe high over my head and drove it into the partly thawed muck. With each thud, a chunk of soil broke away. After I tossed aside the lumps of soil, ice, and moss, I moved the point to a new location and continued the process of thawing and digging.

By six o'clock it was becoming dark and I found it more and more difficult to see what I was doing. When I mentioned my predicament, Sally reported that she had just filled the boiler with water—we couldn't stop now.

"I'll go to the cabin and see what Jerry has to say," I offered. Ten minutes later I made my way back up the hill, stumbling along the uneven trail in the snow. Pausing to catch my breath, I looked up at the boiler. Sally was checking the firebox, and a bright orange glow spread across the snow. Sparks shot up from the smokestack, etching the dark sky with streaks of red. Even from partway down the hill, I could hear the chugging and hissing of the steam.

I found Sally resting in the snowbank, watching the pressure gauge. "What did he say?" she asked.

"He said that the miners would have worked with lamps until the water was used up. Too bad we brought our headlamps!"

Even with a lamp I found it difficult to see anything in the pit. The steam created such a dense cloud of fog when it met the cold air I thought I was in a new type of Turkish steam bath.

"Here comes Jerry," Sally reported a while later. I turned to see the bobbing of a headlamp as he climbed the path.

"I brought some supper. Let's take a break," he said, uncovering a platter. "Moose burgers on homemade bread." Hungry from the day's work outdoors, we devoured the mountainous burgers.

"You're getting there," Jerry said, peering down into our pit. It was now almost waist deep.

"You might as well call it quits when the boiler runs dry. I'll bring up some sheets of tin roofing so we can cover the hole," he added.

It was well after nine o'clock by the time we'd used up the water and the fire had burned out. Working by headlamp, I dug out the last of the loosened and thawed soil. I wanted to remove as much material as possible—there was no point in cutting more wood to thaw the same dirt again tomorrow.

Once the pit was cleared we covered the hole with the sheets of metal. Jerry told us that old-timers would have covered their holes with wood and moss to insulate the pits for the night.

Exhausted, we stumbled down to Jerry's cabin. We chatted with Jerry awhile before continuing down the hill to the cabin in the valley. As soon as my head hit the makeshift pillow of my down parka, I was asleep.

Sally and I returned the following morning. As usual, we stopped at the cabin to chat over tea. It was early afternoon by the time we started cutting wood, and after three when we fired up the boiler.

As we'd done the day before with Jerry, we started with a small fire to warm the boiler, then added a little water to check that everything was working properly. Finally, I tested the pressure release valve to ensure it was not frozen closed.

This time I kept the steam point in each hole for a longer time, allowing the steam to penetrate the frozen ground. Slowly, steadily, I thawed downward in a three-foot-wide circle. Soon we were working in the low light of dusk again. It was early March and the hours of daylight were still limited.

In between stoking the bonfires in his test pits, Jerry came by to check on our progress.

"It's really neat working with steam in a deep pit," Jerry said. "When you come to the surface all the moisture on you freezes instantly and your face turns completely white. Only problem was many miners got pneumonia from inhaling all that steam at forty below!"

Jerry suggested that we use up the steam we had, then cover the hole for a couple of hours. The warmth held in by the sheet metal would continue thawing the ground while we took a break.

Sally and I had just shut the boiler down when we heard a loud clanging from the direction of the cabin. It was Jerry banging gold pans together to announce that supper was ready. We drained the remaining water out of all the pipes so they wouldn't freeze, then headed down to the cabin for a well-earned rest.

At ten o'clock we returned with headlamps. I climbed down into the hole with a shovel. The cover had held in a surprising amount of heat and the soft mud at the bottom of the pit almost came to the top of my borrowed rubber boots. The water-saturated soil, combined with rocks, was so heavy I was unable to heave more than half a shovelful to the lip of the pit. Any deeper and we would need to rig up a windlass to haul up the muck.

"Make sure you dump the dirt out of the way so we don't have to move it again later," Jerry advised, obviously enjoying the role of supervisor.

Sally and I spent an hour digging out the thawed dirt. Then Jerry suggested we take samples from the pit.

"Could you fill this bag with sand from just below the black soil?" Jerry asked, passing a rock hammer and a small cloth bag down to me.

I scraped soil from different layers of the pit into several numbered bags. The first sample was near the surface. The next came from a vein of gravel, and on down to a seam of clay-like soil. The six-foot-deep hole gave Jerry a good cross-section of soil samples. By panning each layer separately, Jerry would learn where any gold was located.

In the early hours of the morning we sat in Jerry's cabin and prepared to pan out the samples. In the centre of the cabin floor, taking up most of the available space, was a metal tub filled with clean water.

"Now I see what you meant by washing water," Sally said. "I thought you were getting water to do your laundry when we met you."

"Nope. It's for washing my gold!"

Since Sally was eager to try her hand at panning, Jerry handed her a gold pan.

"Sink that pan right in the water," he encouraged Sally. She plunged the dirt-filled pan into the tub, then stirred the dirt with her fingers.

"You can scoop those out," Jerry said, pointing to the bark, needles, and moss that had floated to the surface.

"I think you'd better show me the right way to pan," Sally said a few minutes later.

Jerry put on a pair of rubber gloves, explaining that he had an ailment common to many miners—arthritis in his hands. It's a result, he said, of spending too many hours panning with his hands immersed in icy-cold creeks and working barehanded on machinery in frigid temperatures.

He immersed the gold pan into the water, lifted it out, then sloshed the pan from side to side.

"You can do it many ways. Some people swirl. I jiggle," he said. We watched as Jerry worked quickly and efficiently, his motions smooth from years of practice.

"Keep it moving or the contents become solid. You want the gold to sink to the bottom."

He jiggled the pan, then tipped it to let the water flush out some of the material. "This is called fanning," he said, repeatedly dipping the edge of the pan into the water.

"The gold is at the bottom. I won't lose any," he explained when Sally gasped as a handful of sand washed over the edge. Wordlessly, he reached into the pan and plucked out a shiny, golden cube. He handed it to Sally.

Her eyes shone with excitement as she held the cube in her hand. I could see she was mentally calculating how much it might be worth, when Jerry bumped her hand, seemingly by accident. Sally looked horrified when the cube fell into the tub of water.

"Oops," he said, then looked up with a wide grin. "Ha ha, tricked you. It's fool's gold!" he exclaimed. Jerry then told us that the golden cube was actually iron pyrite. Many novice prospectors were fooled by these gold-like crystals.

"I knew that," I interjected quickly.

"Then how come you jumped towards the tub?" Jerry countered, rubbing his whiskers to hide the grin we could hear in his voice.

Sally gave a resigned sigh and returned to panning— jiggling and tipping and fanning and jiggling and swishing. Jerry and I talked, leaving Sally to work in peace.

"You can be a bit more aggressive," Jerry said after Sally had been panning for half an hour. There seemed to be a lot of material still in her pan.

"You have to keep a picture in your mind of the gold always settling to the lowest part of the pan," Jerry added.

"But each time I let gravel wash out I expect some gold to wash out too!" Sally said anxiously. She stepped up her pace, and an extra few grains of sand per minute washed over the top.

"Let's see what's in the pan," I suggested impatiently a short time later.

Jerry showed Sally how to swirl the pan in a circular motion, letting the sand swish around the pan. The contents settled around the bottom, in a line of colours ranging from tan sand to brown iron oxide to black magnetite.

"Hey, there's some gold mixed with that black stuff!" Sally called out.

I leaned over Sally's shoulder to have a look. The gold was heavy and hadn't travelled far around the pan. It sat in a thin line, sparkling in the lamplight. We'd been in the Yukon for months and this was the first time we'd seen gold in a pan. I wondered how many stampeders had struggled all the way to the Klondike only to leave the north without ever seeing this.

"Keep panning. When you're down to just the black sand and gold, I'll pull the black sand out with a magnet."

When Jerry had removed most of the magnetite, he placed the pan on the stove to dry the sand. Two cups of tea later, the contents of the pan were dry and he tipped the material into a triangular copper tray. Gently, he blew across the tray. Dust-sized particles of sand flew into the air until mostly gold remained.

Jerry set out his scale and weighed the grains of gold. "That's about four dollars' worth. I'll put it in a vial for your wages!"

Sally missed the joke. Instead, she looked up, thrilled at the offer of gold. "Thanks, that's the first gold I've ever panned," she said. It could have been four hundred dollars' worth from the look on Sally's face.

"It's not much. After all, we only dug a test pit," Jerry said. "I didn't really expect to see anything in this pan; let's try the next sample."

At that late hour, we happily let Jerry pan the rest of the samples. It took him only four or five minutes for each pan. This way, we would get some sleep before dawn.

"Well," he said after panning the last sample. "There's not much gold there, and hardly any quartz. I'll try another pit higher up the hill."

He handed Sally the gold from the first pan. At least there was something to show for our efforts!

This was our last night with Jerry. As a special treat before continuing our journey, we feasted on a late-night snack of salmon steaks from his larder.

"Thanks for your hospitality," Sally said. "Now we know all about the glamorous life of mining in winter. We'll think of you digging pits during the next snowstorm."

With heavy toboggans in tow, Sally and I continued on our snowshoe trip. After reaching the Yukon River, we headed towards Whitehorse, following much of the route we had taken by scow the previous summer. In stretches where fast water made the ice unsafe, we snowshoed along the overland route.

We enjoyed the rhythm of trail life, especially when the temperature moderated to a balmy twenty degrees Fahrenheit. With the warmer weather, the snow became less granular and the toboggans actually slid with "barely a tugging reminder."

After three weeks of travelling through soft spring snow we set up our last camp on the shore of Lake Laberge, where we had built our scow seven months earlier. As we sat by the campfire that evening, our thoughts turned from snowshoeing back to mining. The snow was dwindling fast and Sally and I were eager to return to the gold-fields.

"Remember what Jerry said—we should come back in the spring when he's sluicing," Sally reminded me. I knew what was coming next.

Sally took a deep breath and continued. "I just know we'll see lots of gold. He even told us to bring our gold pan!"

NINETEEN

Rockers and Riffles

By the end of April, ice and snow in the Klondike was dwindling and the creeks were starting to flow, fed by meltwater from the receding snow. With spring run-off not far away, we were eager to return to Upper Bonanza Creek and visit Jerry Bryde.

Sally and I walked up the mountain towards Seven Pup, taking the route we had snowshoed six weeks earlier. As we climbed towards Jerry's claim we discovered that spring was not nearly as advanced as in the valley. The snow was still knee-deep although we were able to walk on the icy trail, which had been packed by use through the winter.

We found Jerry just outside his cabin, panning in a tub of water. He greeted us with that wonderful grin of his.

"Hello, you claim jumpers!" he called out. His cap was pushed back at a crooked angle leaving his long curly hair poking out. "Whatcha been up to? Did you go on your trip, or did you hibernate somewhere?"

"We snowshoed to Whitehorse, hauling our sleds like the Klondikers," I answered.

"In melting snow? Three hundred miles?" Jerry said, looking at us in disbelief.

"In toboggan-eating snow," Sally said, rolling her eyes.

"Sounds like it was a tough slog!" Jerry exclaimed.

"It was," I agreed. Our backs were still sore. Hand mining would be a breeze after that.

We sat on chairs in the snow, enjoying the warmth of the sun and the view of Upper Bonanza Creek valley. Over several cups of tea and a plate of goodies, we shared stories of our snowshoe trip. We also learned of Jerry's recent activities. Jerry had continued digging test pits and now had a good idea where quartz veins traversed the hillside.

During the past six weeks, much of the snow had melted. Now we could see objects that had been buried in March. On an outside wall of the cabin was a collection of old shovels, pickaxes, rakes, and pitchforks found in the area. Work-worn wheelbarrows, sluiceboxes, and other mining tools were arranged about the yard.

"I've found quite a collection of tips for pickaxes," Jerry said. "I think miners broke the tips off when they tried to pry apart the bedrock. They could see the gold in the cracks so I bet they were really frustrated when they couldn't get it!"

Jerry held a well-worn shovel in his hands. "I've always wanted to learn more about the people who owned these tools," he continued. "This winter, I followed up on some detective work I did at the mining recorder's office."

Jerry had been busy writing letters and he shared the results of his research. He had learned that in 1901, this claim had belonged to Philip Holloway, who had come to the Klondike from Wiltshire, England.

"And guess which route Philip Holloway followed to get here?" Jerry asked. He left a long pause, smiling as we leaned forward for the answer. "He came up the Stikine Trail."

"That means we followed his footsteps up the Stikine Trail, *and* ended up here." I wondered if perhaps it had been more than a coincidence that we had met Jerry in March.

Jerry must have guessed what I was thinking. "Maybe one of those Klondike spirits you've been talking about guided you here," he said with a smile.

In a letter from Mr. Holloway's granddaughter, Jerry learned that Philip had immigrated to Canada in 1898 and joined the North-West Mounted Police. Accompanying the letter was a faded photograph of Philip standing ramrod-straight in his uniform.

Sally and I studied the photograph, trying to get a sense of the character of the person on the faded sepia print. I tried to imagine what it might have been like to be a police officer in the Klondike. They worked for meagre wages, surrounded by people who were staking claims on the creeks and becoming as rich as kings. Eventually, Philip caught the Klondike fever and received his discharge to seek his fortune in the gold-fields. Records show he had staked claims on Seven Pup in May 1901 and worked the claims until 1912.

Jerry had come across many places where Philip had worked. He could see the trenches and the tailing piles, as well as the test pits where Philip had also tried to plot the quartz veins.

"I feel as though I know him," Jerry continued. He paused, gazing across the hillside with a faraway look. "I wonder if I'll do as well as he did." Philip's granddaughter had written that Philip had found enough gold to buy a large farm in southern British Columbia.

"In many ways, he was like me. He didn't like to work with partners." Jerry had learned that Philip's first and only partner went to Dawson one day to sell their gold and was never heard from again.

"Sometimes I can feel the presence of the miners before me. When I find a shoe I place my foot beside it. Going by the shoes and this walking stick," he said, leaning lightly on a hand-carved cane, "I'd say Philip was about my height."

Jerry enjoyed learning about the past and had already discovered much about Philip by uncovering relics and going through his dump. Judging by the number of tins buried in one place, Jerry concluded that Philip must have been doing very well—poor miners did not eat tinned meat.

We continued looking at artifacts Jerry had collected over the years. Jerry had found old pots and pans, liniment bottles, and even a pocket watch buried in the moss.

Then Jerry took us on a tour of the largest relics in his historical collection. Several hulking machines were arranged about the yard, including pumps, boilers, and steam engines.

"That vertical steam engine gave Philip a lot of trouble. It has a patchwork of nuts and bolts and plates holding it together."

Sally and I looked at the rusting equipment from a new perspective. Each pump, each steam engine represented the history of Seven Pup. Like the boiler we had used in March, some were still in working condition.

Jerry continued his tour by taking us up the hill behind his cabin. He stopped to show us where a slight depression and a swath of willow bushes cut a straight line through the spruce forest. After we puzzled over this unusual growth of willows, Jerry told us that Philip had dug a mile-long trench by hand to bring water to the claim. During spring run-off, the trench had brought water to holding ponds for use later in the season when water was scarce.

"Water is almost as valuable as gold up here. That's why no one else had worked this claim since Philip," Jerry said. Like Philip, Jerry had learned to work with the water that was available.

I looked up the hill and saw only a few trickles of water running down the sun-warmed slope. Spring run-off had not yet started at this elevation.

Jerry followed my gaze. "There isn't enough water for sluicing yet, but there is enough to use a rocker box," he said. He pointed up the hill to a wooden box with a shovel propped against it.

"Like to see how it works?" he asked. We needed no more prompting and climbed the hill for a demonstration.

Jerry shovelled in some dirt and added a scoop of water from a tub beside the rocker, then began rocking the contraption. The weather-beaten rocker box creaked rhythmically as Jerry pushed, then pulled the wooden handle. Water sloshed over the top with each thrust, and rocks rattled out of the discharge chute.

The wooden box looked so much like a cradle that I almost expected an infant to be nestled inside. Only the sight of Jerry heaving a shovelful of pay dirt into the top broke the illusion.

The rocker box was three feet long by one foot wide, with a set of curved planks, called "rockers," attached to the bottom. At one end of the unit was a square box, topped with a removable tray featuring a perforated sheet-iron bottom. This tray, called a "grizzly," separated large rocks from the mix of dirt and gravel.

Below the tray, stretched diagonally from the top to the bottom of the box, was an apron of canvas. A gap was left at the lower end of the canvas for dirt and water to flow out the discharge chute.

"If you had been digging shafts all winter," Jerry explained, "you would have a pile of dirt waiting to be worked with a rocker like this."

Jerry left us to try the rocker on our own. Sally started to shovel soil into the top energetically. Using a tin can nailed to the end of a long stick for a ladle, I scooped water from the tub and poured it onto the soil in the tray. I gripped the handle firmly and started rocking the box. Water splashed over the top, into my boots. The one thing I'll remember about the Klondike experience was that it always seemed to involve wet feet.

"Wait!" I protested. "That's way too much dirt. Let me wash some through." Sally scooped a shovelful out and I tried again.

With one hand I poured in scoops of water and with the other I rocked the cradle. Now the rocker box was working properly. The water loosened the dirt, dissolving it so the sand and soil and the smallest stones washed through the holes of the grizzly. This material continued down across the apron of canvas and out the rectangular discharge chute. Any nuggets would remain lodged on the canvas while the smaller particles of gold would wash farther down. The gold would be trapped behind raised strips of wood, called riffles, in the discharge chute.

"Okay, you can add more dirt now," I said to Sally. I was kept busy rocking the box with my left hand and scooping water with my right hand. It was like rubbing my stomach and patting my head at the same time.

After a few more shovelfuls, the grizzly became clogged with rocks too large to pass through the holes. Sally dumped the rocks onto a pile beside us, then we continued our routine. Slowly, the pile of rocks grew.

"Do you think there's any gold in there yet?" Sally asked hopefully when Jerry came by a short time later.

"I doubt it. You've hardly moved any material," he said.

I had to agree that the pile of washed rocks didn't look very large. This system was faster than panning, although it wasn't what I would call production mining.

Over the next four hours we settled into the rhythm of working the rocker: shovel, add water, rock, dump, shovel, add water, rock, dump. Once again, I checked the apron for nuggets of gold. Where were all those nuggets that the old guidebooks had said lay on the ground just waiting to be picked up? Where were the seams of gold, like cheese in a sandwich?

Jerry laughed when I shared my thoughts. "Some people thought all you had to do was mix water with dirt and out came gold. It's not quite that easy."

There were just a few small flecks of gold in the rocker, and Jerry told us that we had moved only half a cubic yard of material. A hand-miner would have to move almost ten times that amount each day to make mining worthwhile. For stampeders who came north expecting to just scoop up the nuggets, they certainly had to work hard for every ounce of gold.

"In a couple of weeks there should be enough water to try sluicing," Jerry said at the end of the day. Then, he assured us, we would move more material through the sluicebox to find more gold.

As Jerry predicted, most of the snow on the hillsides on his claim had melted when we returned in mid-May. The meltwater cascaded down the mountain in hundreds of silver rivulets. There was now enough water to start working on a larger scale.

Jerry produced a small sluicebox. We would work on a pile of gold-bearing sand, soil, and gravel that Jerry had pushed into a twelve-foot-high pile the previous fall. He told us that a sluicebox worked on the same principle as a rocker box, but it could process a larger volume with less effort.

We worked together to set the sluicebox in place. Like the rocker it was handmade from wood. Three boards formed a six-foot-long trough for water and dirt to run through.

"We need some rocks under that far side to shim it up," Jerry said as we wiggled the sluicebox into position on the hillside. We adjusted the sluice by digging away the soil or adding rocks until Jerry felt the angle was just right.

Jerry told us that the slope of the sluicebox depended on how much water would be going through the box. There wasn't much water yet, so the angle of the box was quite steep. As the volume of water increased, we would decrease the angle so gold would have a chance to be caught in the riffles.

I helped Jerry put the rest of the sluicebox together. Along its length we placed dense nylon matting, which I recognized as plastic indoor-outdoor carpet. In fact, I'd even seen some on Jerry's doorstep. Jerry laughed and said that when miners discovered this carpet was perfect for using in a sluicebox the price tripled in the Yukon.

We secured a criss-cross grid of metal on top of the matting. This metal formed riffles, which allow the heavy gold to drop and become trapped in the matting. Along each side we bolted on strips of wood to hold the metal securely in place.

I looked at Jerry's sluice and thought of how miners had worked in the old days. They would have made their rockers from wood and nails taken from their scows or

Sally at the rocker box

Using a sluicebox

packing crates. Sluiceboxes, and even the flumes that carried water across the valleys, were installed with some sort of material to trap the gold. Back then, strips of canvas tarpaulin or wool blanket had been used under wooden riffles.

Once Jerry's sluicebox was in place, we went in search of moss.

"I don't know what miners would have done without moss!" Jerry said as we gathered up armfuls of the soggy vegetation. "They used it for everything—chinking their cabins, plugging cracks in sluiceboxes, and even sealing leaks in their pumps. I've found several places where Philip had stockpiled moss around his claim."

Jerry stuffed moss under the leading edge of the sluice to prevent water from leaking under the box. He explained that even now moss was the best material for sealing gaps; the moss was everywhere and the price was right.

While Jerry and I arranged a funnel of boulders to direct water into the sluice, Sally built a dam to create a settling pond at the end of the trough. Here, the silt would have a chance to settle before the water continued down the hill.

Sally was dressed for the job in rubber gloves and the knee-high rubber boots she had worn during our scow trip. She dropped a boulder into the pond, and mud splashed up, soaking her. She looked up at me with a crooked grin, as if caught playing in the mud while wearing her best clothes.

"Now I know what it was like for you last summer in the swamps!" she said, wiping mud from her face. I laughed as I remembered our journey. Our muddy days on the trail had prepared us well for muddy days on the claim.

"Hey, you two. Let's alter that flow of water to the sluice," Jerry called over, pointing to the water coursing down the hill. He attacked the ground with a shovel to divert a stream of water towards the sluicebox. The water cut its way into the hill, carrying down mud and sand and rocks.

Using a hoe, Jerry pulled dirt into the gully, letting the flow of water break the clumps apart and carry the material into the sluice.

"Nothing to it!" he said as we watched dirt and gravel flow over the riffles. It was a simple process, using gravity and the spring run-off to move material through the sluice. At the end of the day, Sally and I headed down to the valley and left Jerry to work on his own.

When Sally and I returned to Seven Pup a week later, in late May, spring run-off was at its peak. Now there was almost too much water washing down the hill. To keep the sluice working properly, we had to hustle—guiding the flow of water, moving boulders, and breaking up chunks of frozen soil. As it was a hundred years ago, the spring run-off was the busiest time of the mining season. It was a time when miners worked long hours to take advantage of the abundant water.

"I think I'll leave you two working here. I can set up another sluicebox nearby and take some of that water," Jerry said. By diverting the water and splitting the flow, we were able to double our production. Sally and I worked on one sluice and Jerry on another.

"You can see why I like working up here," he said during one of our breaks. "The water does most of the work, from washing down the hillside to carrying away the rocks at the other end. Down in the valley, miners had to do a lot more shovel-work."

Even with the help of the water, Sally and I had to work quickly. It seemed that as soon as we turned our backs, rocks and sand built up in a pile over the riffles. These blockages caused the water, and the gold, to cascade over the sides of the box instead of becoming trapped in the matting. I was supposed to maintain a constant flow of water and material to give the gold a chance to settle behind the riffles.

My job was to control the amount of material entering the sluicebox. Sally stood below the sluice, watching the discharge chute. She was kept busy with a hoe, pulling sand and gravel through the chute so it didn't back up and flood our work area.

"You're getting the hang of it. I'll make miners out of you

yet!" Jerry said when we headed back to his cabin.

This day, as on our previous visits, Sally and I trudged back down the mountain with tired, heavy steps . . . and big smiles.

By early June the peak of the spring run-off was over. Fortunately, Jerry had captured a considerable amount of water in two holding ponds so he could continue working through the summer.

"Now we can put some material through the big sluicebox," Jerry said. "If you help me drag it up the hill, we can get to work!"

I winked at Sally. Hadn't we heard that before?

TWENTY

Using a Monitor

"A little to the left," Jerry grunted as we heaved against the heavy steel sluicebox. Sally and I helped wiggle the sluicebox into position using a combination of muscle power and crowbars. Then we wedged boulders under one corner to level the box from side to side.

"We'll have to run water through to test it," Jerry said, kneeling to check if the box was level. "That's the only way to know for sure if it's right."

We had set up the twelve-foot-long sluice where Jerry decided he'd like to work for a few seasons. This is what he had been working towards since February. After many test pits during the winter and several small sluicing operations during the spring run-off, Jerry had chosen the most productive ground.

Jerry had selected his claim well. In addition to having a promise of gold, it featured several springs. His main water supply was from high above him. Instead of using a long trench as Philip Holloway had, Jerry directed the water through a pipe hundreds of feet down the hill to where we would work.

"Everywhere I work, I find reminders that Philip was

here before me," Jerry said. "It's as if we came to the same conclusions." He pointed to a rusted metal pipe leading from one of the springs. Even now, decades after it had been last used, water still trickled from the end of the pipe.

"I've also found sections of stove-pipe hooked together and used as water pipes," Jerry added. "And just below the tub I use to control the water flow to my sluice, is a box that Philip used."

Jerry led us to an old wooden box, still sitting where it had been used long ago. The box was fitted with an outflow pipe at the bottom and an inlet pipe at the top. I looked up to Jerry's metal tub—in many ways, it was a twin of the old one. One pipe from the spring fed into it. Another pipe protruded from the bottom, and a large-diameter hose carried the water down the hill to where we would be working. No wonder Jerry felt he could sense Philip's presence as he worked.

Sally and I laid out a series of hoses to connect with the flow of water from the galvanized tub. Near the sluice, we attached the hose to a nozzle mounted on a waist-high swivel base. This unit, called a monitor, would allow us to direct a high-pressure stream of water onto the hillside. Jerry told us that this method of using water to wash material into sluiceboxes was called hydraulic mining. This system had been used by miners for decades before the Klondike gold rush.

Before starting work with the monitor, we needed to rig up a discharge flume to direct the flow of material from the sluice down to the settling pond. We decided to build old-style wooden flumes.

"Hey, we could use planks from your scow just as the stampeders did," Jerry suggested.

"Can't—our scow has flowers growing in it now," Sally replied. She explained that we had given the scow to friends in Dawson. They had dragged it into their yard to be used as an oversized flower box.

Instead, we collected weathered planks from a collapsed building nearby. Sally set to work pulling out nails and stacking the planks while I hammered each nail straight so that it could be reused. Although the nails were rusted, they were in good enough condition for this project. I was surprised that some were actually square-sided horseshoe nails, not carpentry nails.

"Reminds me of reshoeing Mare," Sally said, hammering one of the horseshoe nails into a board as we started building the flume.

"At least you don't have to worry about which way the bevel goes," I replied.

The key to building the flume was to make each twelve-foot section interlocking. We narrowed one end of each base plank so it would fit into the next section of flume. After nailing the sides on, we had a long wooden trough braced with crosspieces. It took us the full day to build ten lengths of flume.

Once we had dragged each section up the hill to the sluicebox, we began joining them together. With Jerry's help, we elevated the first section with a barrel and boulders until it was waist-high and level with the end of the sluicebox. Using more boulders, planks, and endless blocks of wood, we adjusted the height of each section until the flume descended at a steady grade. Then we stuffed moss into gaps at the joints to prevent water and muck from leaking out.

We stood back to admire our handiwork. A line of grey troughs curved from the sluicebox down to the settling pond, looking just like the ones we had seen in the old photographs. Our engineering feat brought to mind one image of Bonanza Creek where flumes criss-crossed the valley from claim to claim.

Those were the glory days of the Klondike, when the first gold was gleaned from the rich ground. I closed my eyes and conjured up an image of glittering, gleaming gold. Ahhh, handfuls of nuggets clogging the sluice!

"Well, let's run some water through the box," Jerry said, bringing me back to reality.

Jerry took the first turn with the monitor. Using the spray

of high-pressure water, Jerry carved a gully into the hillside, to direct the flow of material to the sluicebox.

"Now that we have a 'cut' we can work a wider area," Jerry shouted over the din of splashing water.

Except for the monitor, the principle was the same as using the spring run-off—a flow of water carried rocks and mud through the sluice. If the sluice was set up correctly, any gold would be caught by the riffles and the remaining rocks and mud would be carried through to the tailings flume.

Sally took over while Jerry and I went to check on the holding pond. Jerry left her with instructions not to let any large boulders or a landslide of material wash into the sluicebox.

"Be careful, or you'll wipe out the box and lose all the gold!" he said with loud emphasis. His warning would have been more daunting if Sally hadn't caught him glance at me and smile.

When I took my turn at the monitor I discovered it was a wet job. The spray pounded against the rocks, splashing me with muddy droplets of water. It was then I remembered reading that miners during Klondike times were always wet from standing in ponds, working monitors, and panning gold. I had wanted to know how it felt to be a miner and now I knew—it was uncomfortably wet.

I swept the jet of water back and forth, watching for any clumps of earth that might tumble down to the sluice. Then, despite all my efforts, I saw a tidal wave of mud and gravel bearing down on me. Remembering what Jerry had done, I directed the water into the wall of mud to slow it down and break it up. I was too late. The mudslide had too much volume and momentum.

"Break up that slurry!" Jerry called down to me. I sensed the urgency in his voice but didn't know what to do. In a flash Jerry jumped into the cut and stood in the path of the flood. The wall of black mud hit his legs, threatening to wash over his knee-high boots. The mudslide slowed. Then it broke up, working its way slowly around his legs like a thick soup.

"There are a hundred ways to lose gold—and a slurry is one of them," Jerry said. He explained that the gold would be carried through the sluice, suspended in the thick slurry of mud and gravel.

"Don't worry; it's happened to me many times. You won't be a real hand-miner until you've wiped out a gold-filled sluicebox, fallen into the mud, and stepped on your glasses," Jerry said, laughing. "A good disaster now and then keeps life interesting."

I continued sluicing, gradually becoming more competent as the day wore on. The rocks rattled over the metal entrance to the sluice, then clattered over the riffles and rumbled down the discharge flume towards the tailings pile.

"I love that sound," Jerry said, listening to the steady flow of rocks rolling through the sluice. "It's music to my ears."

Sally was the "box tender," a term used during the gold rush days for the person who looked after the sluicebox. Jerry had said that if rocks became lodged in the sluice, the resulting turbulence would prevent the gold from settling into the mats. Yet another way to lose the gold, I realized. Sally also had to keep an eye on the discharge flume. Each time it became blocked with gravel, she had to rush down and shovel it out.

After an hour of sluicing, we shut off the monitor to allow the warmth of the sun to melt the exposed permafrost. This was a good opportunity to inspect the ground in the cut.

"Notice the smell?" Jerry asked as we worked our way up the cut. It was a rich, earthy odour, slightly reminiscent of being in a barn.

"Rub the soil in your fingers. The smell and feel of this red material is different from the soil at the surface, which is more peat-like." We learned that the red, oxidized material was an indication of what we might find underneath—gold!

"What's this?" Sally asked, picking up a red-tinged rock.

"It's leaverite," Jerry replied, studying the sample closely. He paused for a moment, then continued. "It's not worth

Working with the monitor

Cleaning out the flume

anything. Leaverite where you found it."

Still chuckling over this miner's joke, Jerry stopped mid-stride and picked up a fist-sized chunk of white quartz.

"See where the pyrites have dissolved and fallen out?" he asked, holding out the rock for us to have a look. "That's a good sign gold is nearby. Look at the gold on this side. It's loaded!"

There, on the weathered surface of the quartz, sat several flakes of gold.

"Now you try and find one," he said over his shoulder as he glissaded down the hill. "No supper for you until you find a rock with gold."

We began walking back and forth across the cut, stooping to pick up each lump of quartz. I couldn't believe that the first piece Sally picked up was also loaded with gold. It was weeks before I found one.

As the three of us sat on the edge of the sluicebox, we talked about Jerry's lifestyle. He was suited to this life of mining, where the rhythm of his days was governed by the amount of water available and the depth of permafrost the sun could melt each day. This was not the place for an impatient person; the run-off couldn't be hurried and the weather couldn't be controlled.

Jerry was content with this slower pace of life. With it came the freedom to live each day as he saw fit, to work when he wanted, and to extract the amount of gold required to meet his needs. He was happy living on the mountain from where he could watch the rest of the world rush by.

"I could live this way," Sally said to no one in particular. I knew what she was feeling. We both understood the lure of a simpler life like the one Jerry was leading. The busy world seemed light years away as we sat gazing across the valley.

"I think I know why Klondikers came all this way," I responded. "Perhaps it wasn't just gold they were looking for; maybe it was freedom."

The three of us sat quietly, each absorbed in our own

thoughts. After several minutes, Jerry broke the silence.

"Well, enough philosophizing," he said. "Let's go play in the mud."

We continued using the monitor for two more days, until the spray lacked enough pressure to bring down new material. It was time to use a pump to boost the pressure, Jerry informed us. With the pump Jerry could recycle the water from holding pond to monitor to settling pond and back again, without having to rely solely on the water running down the hillside. Any loss of water would be made up within a day or two by water flowing from the springs.

The pressure of the pump to the monitor drove the jet of water three times higher than the gravity-fed system had. The water blasted the soil free from the frozen ground and sent a spray of water and mud several feet into the air.

Production was accelerated, but with the greater volume of water and material gushing down the hill came a need to work much faster. While Jerry controlled the monitor, I worked furiously with a pitchfork, tossing out rocks that were too large to enter the sluice. Sally was busy keeping the riffles and discharge flume clear. Just when I was beginning to tire, Jerry throttled the pump to a lower pressure.

"When I'm sluicing by myself I don't bring as much material through the box," Jerry explained. "It's quite a job for one person running the monitor, keeping the box clear, and watching for plug-ups in the flume."

By the time we next visited Seven Pup, Jerry had been sluicing for several days with the high-pressure monitor. It was time for the next stage of hand mining. Jerry explained that while some of the gold would have been washed down to the sluicebox, most of it would have settled on the hillside. As we wandered up the cut, Jerry pointed out several flecks of gold that had dropped into the cracks and crevices. Gold is nineteen times heavier than water and considerably heavier than other minerals, so it settles quickly. The ground itself worked like a sluice. We could see where gold had come to rest in low places, especially where rocks and roots acted like riffles.

Working our way back down, we started picking up the largest rocks and tossing them into buckets.

"Be sure to hit the rocks against each other to knock off any gold," Jerry instructed.

This job was time-consuming and labour-intensive, but it had to be done. These rocks were too big to be flushed down the hill by the water. Left where they were, the rocks would prevent the gold-bearing sand and gravel from washing down to the sluicebox.

"Sally, you can put more than that in Ian's wheelbarrow," Jerry said. "Load it up!" He dumped another bucket of rocks into the barrow, making a towering pile of rocks for me to wheel down the hill.

It became a competition. The challenge was to make the wheelbarrow as full as possible and get it all the way to the pile without tipping the load.

Whooping and hollering, Jerry and I took turns steering the overloaded wheelbarrow down a series of planks to the pile of rocks. Jerry made sure we dumped the rocks into one large, tidy heap. Philip had been just as tidy, judging by the moss-covered mounds of stacked tailings around the claim.

"Next step is to bring down the gold," Jerry announced. Using a hoe, he scraped down the loose gravel remaining in the cut.

With the gravel came finer material—and gold, Jerry assured us, though we couldn't actually see it. He carefully scraped what he could out of each crack where gold would have settled. When Jerry had finished "bringing down the gold," as he called this procedure, there was a knee-high mound of dirt and gravel at the entrance of the sluice.

Jerry handed Sally a pitchfork with ten narrowly spaced tines. "Your job is to make sure no rocks larger than an egg enter the sluice. Good luck," he added.

It was especially important at this stage, we learned, that only fine gravel be permitted to enter the sluicebox. Larger rocks would carry gold through with them. Jerry operated the monitor at much less pressure than when running raw material through the sluice. I was appointed to keep the riffles and discharge flumes clear.

We repeated the process of bringing down the gold three times; monitoring, tossing out rocks, scraping down the gravel, and sluicing again. Each time, Jerry took a sample of the ground and panned it out to see if there was any gold left behind. Finally, he was satisfied we had claimed most of the gold.

We shut off the pump and waited for the water to drain out of the sluicebox. There, in the dark matting at the top of the riffles, lay several streaks of glittering gold. What a sight!

"Looks like a bonanza!" Jerry said, smiling broadly. "Time for a clean-up."

TWENTY-ONE

The Clean-Up

"Any nuggets?" Sally asked, peering over Jerry's shoulder as he scraped the matting with a finger.

"Yup," he said. "I knew there would be some nice specimens here." Jerry picked up a nugget and handed it to Sally.

"It's beautiful," she said, studying the penny-sized piece of gold in her palm. It was the largest nugget Sally had ever held.

"When Philip worked here," Jerry said, "I'm sure he found many nuggets like that one. But I guess he missed a few!"

Sally placed the nugget back in the uppermost mat, then we helped Jerry release the braces holding the metal riffles in place. After tapping each riffle clean, we set it aside.

"I keep the mats in order, to learn where the gold has settled in the sluice. I call it 'reading the box,' " Jerry informed us.

Ideally, the gold would be trapped in the top two mats. Based on where the gold was, Jerry would adjust the slope of the sluicebox, the amount of material fed into the box, or the volume of water in order to improve the efficiency of his operation.

Each mat, packed with wet concentrates, weighed twenty pounds or more. With great care, we carried them to the cabin where everything was ready for the clean-up. Just outside the cabin was a circle of chairs arranged around two large tubs of water—one for cleaning the mats and one for panning.

I took the uppermost mat and started to wash it clean in a tub. I swished it, wiggled it, and finally slapped the mat aggressively onto the water to dislodge all the trapped material. The mat was large and awkward to work with. By the time I was finished, I was wet from head to toe.

We poured most of the water out of the tub and scooped the concentrates into a gold pan. The concentrates contained a great deal of fine gravel, so Jerry used a series of screens to separate the coarser material. Sally and I were given the task of checking the contents of each screen for nuggets or pieces of quartz with gold embedded in them. Using tweezers, we picked out each likely looking piece and studied it carefully. Before long, we had set aside a thimble-sized mound of nuggets from the first two screens. The next screens yielded fewer nuggets, but the mound still looked impressive to us.

Jerry started to pan the remaining concentrates. With precision that came from doing it thousands of times, he sloshed and jiggled the pan, then let the top layer of gravel wash over the rim. With no pause in the rhythm he continued moving the pan.

We enjoyed watching Jerry work with the gold pan. His every motion was smooth and efficient. "It's not enough to be fast," he said, looking up. "You have to recover all the gold as well."

Jerry paused for a moment and watched the contents of the pan settle. Then he held the pan flat and swirled the material around the bottom. I looked over his shoulder and saw several distinct patterns of colour: white quartz, greyish barite, and black magnetite. At the edge of the black sand was a yellow mass of material. Gold!

"Hey! No peeking," he said, quickly moving the pan again

so that the gold disappeared.

Sally and I took up the challenge, and we begged and wheedled until Jerry conceded.

"Well, I guess you can have a look," he said, flashing a grin. Jerry swirled the pan again and the gold formed another line of yellow. Sally and I had never seen so much gold in a pan before. In fact, we had never seen any gold in our battered pan.

In descending order of size, Jerry explained there were nuggets, clunkers, coarse gold, fine gold, and dust.

"What's a clunker?" Sally asked. Jerry answered her question by picking up a pea-sized nugget and dropping it back into the pan. It landed with a satisfying clunk.

We leaned closer to look at the yellow metal. I studied some pieces with a magnifying loupe and was fascinated to discover a world of triangular crystals and multi-branched specimens that looked like microscopic, golden candelabras. The gold was still sharp-edged and unworn because it had not travelled far. Gold on Jerry's claim had come from quartz veins that cut through Seven Pup, or from other veins just uphill on the Lone Star claim.

"Now it's your turn to pan, Sally, but use your own gold pan," Jerry said. "You swirl the dirt around so much, I'm worried you'll wear mine out!" Sally filled our battered pan with concentrates and immersed it in the tub. She began shaking and sloshing the mixture about.

Eventually, she worked the material down to a few tablespoons of heavy sand mixed with the gold. Jerry put more water in the pan, then used a magnet to pull out the black magnetite.

When all the magnetite was removed, Jerry carefully tipped the water out, then placed the pan in the warm sun to dry the remaining material. Later, he poured the contents into the triangular blow tray that we had seen him use in the winter.

Jerry blew gently across the tray. Out flew some sand, tiny bits of quartz, and other material.

"Now we're left with mostly gold. Let's weigh it," he said,

taking his scale from a shelf in the cupboard. "Place your bets on how many grams we have here."

Our estimates ranged from three to ten grams. Later, we learned that a pinch of gold is approximately one gram, and there are thirty-one grams to a troy ounce. Each gram was worth almost thirteen dollars.

"You guys did a lot of the work," he said, "so we'll divide the gold from this pan three ways." Maybe we would return home with a poke full of gold after all!

Carefully, Jerry poured the gold into the centre of the plate. He adjusted the weights on the scale until the needle remained steady in the centre.

"Five and a half grams," Jerry stated. It didn't surprise me that his estimate of six grams was the closest.

We continued panning out the rest of the concentrates until Jerry had more than a teaspoon of gold. The scales indicated that this clean-up yielded slightly more than an ounce of the precious yellow metal.

"What do you do with the gold now?" I asked.

"Well, I pick out the interesting crystals for my collection. The rest I melt down and sell to one of the gold buyers." He told us that by melting the gold, he removed most of the impurities and received a higher price from the gold buyers.

Sally and I watched as Jerry prepared to melt his gold. He poured the gold into a ceramic crucible. Then, like an alchemist from medieval times, he selected two containers of powder to mix with the gold.

"This is borax. I don't measure it any more, I can just guess how much to add," he said, pouring a generous quantity into the crucible. Then he added a dash of soda ash. Combined with the borax, this would create a flux to absorb impurities from the liquid gold.

Years ago, miners had used coal-burning forges to melt their gold, but Jerry had a small propane-fired furnace. He set the ceramic crucible in the centre of the furnace, then held a match to the jet. With a roar that sounded like a small rocket taking off, the furnace began heating up.

"I like to leave it for half an hour. Let's take a break."

Panning for gold

A good clean-up!

My curiosity drew me back to peek inside before Jerry turned the furnace off. I donned a welding shield to protect my eyes from the intense light and heat. Inside the red-hot furnace, the crucible now contained bubbling yellow liquid.

Even when Jerry announced the gold was "cooked," we had to wait for another half-hour for the molten gold to cool. Slowly, the mass grew darker and darker. When the glass-like material at the top had turned black, Jerry lifted out the crucible with tongs. A sharp whack with a hammer broke the mould and released the gold.

At the bottom was a one-ounce melt of gold, the size and shape of a large coat button. In fact, it was even called a button. But this was no dime-store button—it was worth more than four hundred dollars.

"Now it's time to head to town. I'll pay some bills and buy some groceries. Then we'll go on a 'spree,' as the miners used to call it!" Jerry declared. It was mid-July and he hadn't been off his claim for more than a month.

"I used to be like old-time miners," Jerry said. "After a few weeks up here by myself, I'd long for town. I would set off with my gold poke to buy groceries and other supplies. But somehow I'd return to my cabin a week later, hung over, feeling sick, and unable to work . . . with no groceries and no money."

Jerry assured us that he'd always set out with good intentions. Then, on the way to the grocery store or post office, he would be waylaid by mining friends he hadn't seen for months. One thing would lead to another. . . .

Jerry paused, thinking of the past, then continued. "When I went to the Eldorado Hotel I'd ring the bell and plunk down my poke," he said.

"What bell?" Sally asked.

"Each bar has a bell, something like a large cow bell. If you ring it, it means you're buying a round for everyone in the house."

"That could cost you a lot on a busy night," Sally observed.

"The bar tab was sometimes hundreds of dollars."

As Jerry said, some things hadn't changed since the gold rush. Back then, miners kept a leather poke full of gold to make all their purchases. Gold dust rather than paper money was the currency of the time, and every business had a set of scales.

I remembered reading that a pinch of gold was worth about fifty cents in 1898. One pinch would buy a drink of watered-down whisky. Since the store clerk or bartender did the pinching, those with large fingers were in demand—their pinch was bigger. Other tricks of the trade included long fingernails to surreptitiously scoop up extra gold. Well-greased hair was another ploy. A bartender would pass a hand through his hair before weighing his customer's gold. A certain amount invariably stuck to his greasy fingers, which he wiped on his hair again. Later, the bartender would wash his hair and pan out the gold.

With these stories in mind, Sally and I accompanied Jerry to Dawson the next morning. Our first visit was to a gold buyer. Jerry told us that although the banks buy gold, he preferred to go to one of the independent agents.

Jerry took the button out of his gold poke and gently placed it on the buyer's scale. The scale read 1.05 troy ounces.

The buyer referred to a sheet that indicated gold from Seven Pup had been assayed at seventy-nine percent pure. The rest of the unrefined metal was comprised of silver and other elements. He did a series of calculations based on the price of gold that day and the purity of Jerry's gold. From this figure, the government royalty was subtracted. The royalty rate, strangely enough, had not changed since the turn of the century—it amounted to two and a half percent of the 1898 price of fifteen dollars an ounce. Jerry's royalty payment came to a staggering thirty-nine cents. Finally, the buyer deducted a commission for handling and shipping the gold south for refining.

The buyer weighed another button and repeated the calculations. Then, with a trust that had come from many such transactions, Jerry tucked his receipt and cash into a pocket without checking either.

At the hardware store Jerry pulled his leather poke from one pocket and a set of portable scales from another. He measured out five grams, enough to buy the bits and pieces needed to keep his operation going. Sally and I wondered if there was anywhere else in the world where one customer could pay a bill with a credit card, the next with cash, and another with gold dust.

"Let's visit some bar miners after I've finished my business," Jerry suggested as we clattered along the wooden boardwalk. When Sally asked him who was still mining on the river bars, he laughed and told us the only "bar miners" he knew congregated at the local saloons. We agreed to meet at one of these fine establishments later that afternoon. Jerry assured us he would stock up with groceries to last a few weeks before going on his spree.

When we met Jerry at the Sluice Box lounge, we noticed things that had meant little to us before. Outside the bar hung a sign that read: "Gold Dust Accepted." Inside, secured to a pillar, was the large bell that Jerry had rung on his most memorable spree. The bell was a large brass affair that would ring loudly enough for all in the bar to know the next round was free. Sally restrained me from trying to learn what tone of ring it made!

We met several of Jerry's mining friends in the bar. He introduced us as apprentice hand-miners, which drew a chuckle from everyone. Sally and I found it interesting to hear these miners talk shop. Their problems with loaders and bulldozers needing expensive repairs were so far removed from the challenges facing Jerry. As he said later, when a shovel handle breaks it's not nearly the same catastrophe as when a bulldozer transmission fails.

At ten o'clock that evening, the three of us strolled along the streets taking in the sights. The northern sky wouldn't become dark for several hours yet and few people appeared to be heading home. Like us, most people were walking from one nighttime establishment to another. Music poured out of the wide-open doors of Diamond Tooth Gertie's gambling hall.

Inside, our ears rang with the loud claps, whistles, and stomping of feet. The piano player was pounding out a ragtime tune and the dancers whooped and hollered, adding to the cacophony of sounds. As always, miners threw gambling chips onto the stage to show their appreciation of the singers and scantily dressed dancers.

Even these days, miners come to town to relieve the boredom of working long shifts. With their pockets heavy with gold, they are eager to have a good time and forget all they endured to get the gold!

After a few rounds at the bars and a meal out, it was time to return to the claim. Back at Seven Pup, we relaxed for a day to recover from the excitement of our trip to Dawson. Then it was back to helping Jerry sluice, fix flumes, construct dams, and tackle all the other chores that go with mining. Such was life on the creeks. Not much has changed over the years, after all.

TWENTY-TWO

Staking a Claim

With great ceremony, Jerry awarded Sally and me hand-lettered certificates proclaiming our proficiency as "Hand Miners First Class." It was our last week at Seven Pup, and he announced that our apprenticeship was complete. Then he convinced us that as hand-miners first-class, we could not leave the Klondike without staking a claim.

Studying the placer maps on Jerry's wall, we chose an unstaked area on the upper reaches of Eldorado Creek. Jerry had been there on a prospecting trip and had found a trace of gold.

"Gold? Seams like cheese in a sandwich? Nuggets just waiting to be picked up?" Sally asked, quoting newspaper headlines from gold rush days.

We laughed together at this myth. Sally and I now knew better; finding gold was hard work. Not only that, a miner had to work the claim each year and fill in a mass of paperwork to retain title to it. Even so, we were excited about the idea of having our own claim.

"Well, what are we waiting for?" Sally asked eagerly. "I've wanted to stake a claim all summer!"

The next day, Jerry took us up an unnamed gully that

drained into Eldorado Creek. We trudged up the hill, backpacks loaded with our gold pan, shovel, handsaw, and axe. The Placer Mining Act required us to measure exactly one thousand feet up from the valley floor. There, we blazed the lower claim post.

On the blaze, Sally carefully inscribed: "Post #1. 500 feet upstream to Post #2. Whisky claim. September 9, 1995." Sally wrote her name on the post, then said the name "Whisky" referred to the whisky-jacks, the jays that flew beside us as we climbed the hill. I wasn't entirely convinced that was her real reason.

With visions of gold, I followed Sally up the hill as she paced off the regulation five-hundred-foot claim. Eldorado Creek had some of the richest placer mining ground ever worked—perhaps we would strike it rich after all!

We cleared a path between the two posts as required by the mining regulations, then marked the second claim post. Once these tasks were completed, Jerry helped us choose a likely looking spot in the small creek to see if we could find any gold. Then he left us to pan on our own, to put into practice the skills we had learned through the summer.

I pulled our trail-worn gold pan from the backpack and held it in my hands. It seemed a lifetime ago that we had bought it at the outfitter's store in Vancouver. It was no longer shiny and new.

"Remember these?" I asked Sally, pointing to the pock marks sustained when the pan had fallen off Dusty's load and rattled down the rocky slope, spooking the horses.

"Yeah. The things that pan and you and I went through to get here!"

Every dent told a story. I ran my fingers over a crease in the bottom and remembered where Dusty had crashed into a tree on the Stikine Trail. The bottom was blackened from being used as a frying pan, and a skim of rust was a faint reminder of its application as a bailing vessel for our scow.

I looked over to Sally standing ankle-deep in the mud of the creek. Like the gold pan, we had changed and weathered too. We had been drawn north by the Klondike spirit, and during our journey we had found riches perhaps more elusive than gold. Along the way Sally and I had grown closer as we tackled each new challenge together. We had each discovered an inner strength as we faced the difficulties of bucking broncos, scow-eating rapids, and steep, toboggan-resistant hills.

In some ways, we had lived in the past. However, the memories would last long into our future. Like the Klondikers before us, we had experienced a great adventure, and our lives could never again be quite the same. We had learned that the detours in life often turn out to be more interesting and rewarding than the planned course. If we hadn't been willing to change our plans, we wouldn't have made a new friend and learned all we had from Jerry. Our Klondike journey had also reaffirmed our belief that life should be an adventure.

I leaned over and scooped up a pan of gravel from the creek.

"I see two colours," Sally exclaimed as I finished panning out the fine sands.

"That's a good sign," Jerry said when he wandered over to see how we were doing. "I guess this means you'll be back some day!"

"I guess we will," Sally answered.

FROM THE AUTHORS

Thank you for coming with us to the Klondike. If you grimaced when I rode Blackie through the swamps or held your breath through Five Finger Rapids, then we know you joined with us in reliving the gold rush. We hope you enjoyed reading about our adventures as much as we enjoyed sharing them.

Sally and I would like to invite you to share our other journeys. *Wilderness Seasons* is our story of living in the wilderness of northern British Columbia for fourteen months. Together, we built a log cabin and shared the trials and triumphs of a life far from civilization. This was our first extended trip, and it makes for great fireside reading!

In *Wild and Free,* we tell of our close encounters with wildlife in the north. While Sally got as close as possible to sketch each animal, I peered through a viewfinder to get face-to-snout photographs. Along the way, we were chased by angry bull elk, befriended by porcupines, and had several close encounters with bears and other wild creatures.

Arctic Adventures is the story of our year in the Arctic. We canoed across the Barrens and lived with an Inuit family during early winter. Then, after learning how to handle seven boisterous Huskies, we travelled by dog team down the coast of Hudson Bay, dining by candlelight in igloos and camping on shifting sea ice.

These books span ten years of outdoor adventures and misadventures. If your bookstore doesn't have them on the shelf, we're sure they would be pleased to order them for you.

What's next? Sally's idea is a journey to the coast of northern British Columbia, where, among other things, we would learn how to build a dugout canoe and paddle it down the coast. My notion is to build a birch-bark canoe and follow voyageur routes from Ontario to the Mackenzie River in the Northwest Territories. Either choice sounds like a trip that would have a good dose of adventure along the way!

Ian and Sally Wilson, July 1996

ACKNOWLEDGEMENTS

The following sponsors assisted us with our journey. To all, we are most grateful for their financial assistance, for product contributions, and, most of all, for their faith in our expedition:

Altamira Investment Services for their financial contribution and their enthusiastic support of our expedition.

Hastings Management for their donation, which helped us complete our project.

Klondike Gold Corporation for their assistance and their financial contribution.

Molson Breweries for their support and sponsorship of our adventure.

Richard Hughes for his contribution to our endeavour.

Coleman Canada for supplying us with our Peak 1 camp stoves and Coleman lanterns; these never failed us, even in the coldest weather.

Stanfield's for donating Polartherm as well as wool long johns that kept us warm throughout the long, cold winter.

Lucerne Foods for supporting us with supplies ranging from tinned meats to macaroni dinners.

Far West Industries for their excellent Gore-Tex pants, parkas, and fleece jackets.

Many people helped us along the way. With their support our expedition was everything we had hoped it would be. We would like to thank the following people:

Jerry Bryde for sharing his life on the claim and for teaching us so much about hand mining.

Ray and Reg Collingwood for helping us prepare for the horseback part of our trip, as well as for their generous support while we were in Smithers.

Jennifer Docken in Dawson City for her support.

Julie and Sylvia Frisch and John Lenart in Dawson City for their friendship and for lending us their cozy cabin for the winter.

Tracie Harris for keeping us fueled with sourdough bread while we built our scow at Lake Laberge.

Ed Johnston and Wendy Sudsbear for their hospitality in Dawson City.

Don Knapp for teaching us how to shoe horses.

Jim and Marilyn McCrae for their enthusiasm and tips about horse packing and back-country horse skills.

Italo Sansalone for teaching us how to ride and handle horses.

Slim Sawatsky for teaching us back-country horse skills.

Clyde Westman at Britannia Heritage Shipyard for sharing boat-building tips and for teaching us the art of caulking wooden boats.

Doug and Fran Whittington for their northern hospitality and all their help in Whitehorse.

Bob and Anne Wilson for being our expedition support crew.

The staff at the Yukon Archives for helping with research and for providing historical photographs.

BIBLIOGRAPHY

Our Klondike experience was greatly enhanced by learning about the gold rush before we embarked on our journey. Our book is not a detailed account of the history of the Klondike, and we hope that readers wishing to learn more will find the following material as helpful as we did.

Adney, Tappan. *The Klondike Stampede*. New York: Harper & Brothers Publishers, 1899.

Berton, Pierre. *Klondike*. Toronto: McClelland & Stewart, 1958.

Klondike: The Chicago Record's Book for Gold Seekers. Chicago: Chicago Record, 1897.

Ingersoll, Ernest. *Gold Fields of the Klondike*. Saint John, N.B.: Eagle Publishing House, 1897.

Leonard, John W. *The Gold Fields of the Klondike*. Chicago: A. N. Marquis & Co., 1897.

Ogilvie, William. *The Klondike Official Guide*. Toronto: Hunter Rose Co., 1898.

Rourke, Mike. *Yukon River*. Watson Lake, Yukon: Rivers North Publications, 1985.

INDEX

Also by Ian and Sally Wilson

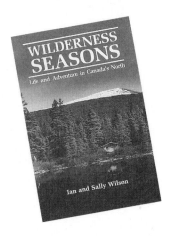

Wilderness Seasons is an inspiring account of a year in remote wilderness, far from the nearest settlement or road. From the challenge of building a hand-hewn log cabin to the intimacy of moose breath at six feet, the authors share the trials and triumphs of a life close to nature.

A NATIONAL BESTSELLER
208 pages, ISBN 0-919574-34-3
$16.95

Wild and Free is a mix of stunning photography, detailed drawings, and personal encounters with wildlife. Mountain climbing with goats, petting porcupines, and meeting burly black bears are just some of the adventures the authors share.

A NATIONAL BESTSELLER
192 pages, ISBN 0-919574-87-4
$16.95

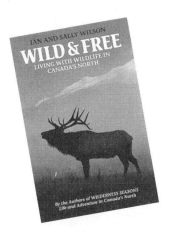

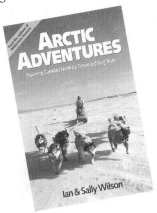

Arctic Adventures is the exciting story of a year-long adventure in the Arctic. The authors travelled 2000 miles by canoe and dog team, lived with an Inuit family, and learned how to build igloos and run a team of seven boisterous Huskies.

A NATIONAL BESTSELLER
248 pages, ISBN 0-919574-43-2
$16.95

Published by Gordon Soules Book Publishers Ltd.